Getting Started in EXPORT

A PRACTICAL GUIDE

ROGER BENNETT

KOGAN
PAGE

First published in 1995

Kogan Page Limited
120 Pentonville Road
London N1 9JN

British Library Cataloguing in Publication Data

A CIP record for this book is available from the British Library.

ISBN 0-7494-1558-4

Typeset by Saxon Graphics Ltd, Derby
Printed and bound in Great Britain by Biddles Ltd, Guildford and King's Lynn

Contents

Preface

With the enlargement of the European Union and the opening up of exciting new markets all over the world there has never been a better time to explore the lucrative opportunities that exporting can provide. It is a sad fact, however, that far too many small businesses enter foreign markets casually and without either the resources or the professional contacts necessary to make their efforts succeed.

This book helps you to take a realistic look at your readiness for exporting, at whether exporting is really for you and, if not, what you might be able to do to modify your products to make them suitable for selling abroad. The text takes you through the entire export process step by step, giving a wealth of advice and practical information on export methods, documentation, legal requirements, insurance and payment procedures, and where to go for further help.

After reading this book you will be in a position to begin exporting to the world's most attractive markets: Western Europe, North America, the English-speaking countries of Australasia and South Africa, and the economic powerhouse of Asia – namely Japan. You should also be able to start thinking constructively about some of the world's more difficult export markets, such as Eastern Europe, Central Africa, and those nations collectively referred to as the 'Third World'. These regions are not covered in the present book, as you will need experience of exporting before attempting to do business in these areas, where foreign exchange shortages, special documentation requirements, barter trading and other complicating factors frequently apply.

My thanks are due to Rosalind Bailey who wordprocessed the manuscript, and to Kogan Page for rapidly expediting the production of the book.

Roger Bennett

Chapter 1
Why Export?

There has never been a better time to start thinking about export. The completion of the European Single Market and the expansion of the EU to incorporate important countries such as Austria, Finland and Sweden have created an abundance of opportunities for selling on the European Continent; while outside Europe the successful conclusion of the most recent round of the GATT negotiations in 1993 has sent tariffs tumbling and is opening up exciting new markets all over the world.

International telephone and fax services to 'remote' regions are vastly better today than they were only a few years ago; facilities for international business travel are extensive; and business service firms (advertising agencies, market research companies, road hauliers, etc) now operate in virtually all nations. Hence, it is much simpler than in the past to visit and examine foreign markets in order to select the most promising, and thereafter to monitor and control your foreign operations.

Trade throughout North and South America is expanding in consequence of the formation of NAFTA (the North American Free Trade Agreement) and through the formation of a number of Central and Latin American Common Markets. A major free trade association is developing in Southern Africa; markets in parts of North Africa and the Middle East are buoyant; and the deal concluded at the Uruguay GATT talks is opening up hitherto inaccessible markets in Southern Asia and throughout the Far East.

You will certainly not be alone if you decide to begin exporting. Britain is the world's fifth largest trading nation, the third largest provider of international commercial services, and exports a quarter of its Gross National Product (compared, for example, with 11 per cent for Japan) each year. You are also fortunate to live in a country possessing some of the most extensive, sophisticated and accessible export support services (international transport firms, shipping agents, export documentation advisors, etc) to be found anywhere in the world.

Reasons for exporting

Benefits from exporting include:

- not having 'all your eggs in one basket'. Business risks can be spread over several countries; if sales decline in one market, they might simultaneously be picking up elsewhere;
- an increased volume of production, enabling you to lower your supply costs and disperse overheads over a greater number of units of output;
- the higher margins that are available in certain foreign markets;
- possibilities for developing a competitive edge here in the UK. The experience and competencies you will acquire through selling abroad are likely to help you beat your domestic rivals. You will develop wider perspectives on customer needs and characteristics, and this should feed through into improved product presentation, packaging and design, more effective distribution and a general improvement of several other aspects of the firm's operations;
- being able to even out the effects of seasonal fluctuations in domestic sales;
- possibly having to face less competition in certain foreign markets than at home;
- a wider customer base. Consumers of your type of product in some foreign markets (especially Continental Western Europe and the USA) may be much wealthier and free-spending than in the UK.

A product that has reached the end of its useful life at home might have a fresh lease of life if introduced to another country. There may be easy access to major customers (via centralised buying by government agencies or retail consortia, for example), and it might be possible to shift slow-moving stock that, while not having succeeded in the home market, might nevertheless be attractive to purchasers abroad. Items that are out of fashion in one country might be highly regarded when introduced elsewhere.

Exporting could become the engine that drives the long-term growth of the firm. It also has a number of advantages as a means for selling abroad when compared with more extensive foreign operations (setting up foreign subsidiaries for example).

There is no risk of the failure of long term foreign investments; the revenues from export sales accrue entirely and directly to yourself; experience of foreign selling is systematically acquired; and you can gradually build up a network of reliable contracts with foreign agents, distributors, retail outlets, and so on. Eventually, this might give you sufficient know-how to launch a more general international marketing effort with your becoming involved in foreign manufacture or assembly, or in the import to one foreign country of goods from a second foreign country for subsequent local sale or re-export; or the establishment of permanent establishments in foreign nations to warehouse and distribute goods.

The problems involved

You might be put off the idea of exporting by the prospects of having to:

- deal with complicated export documentation;
- obtain accurate market information;
- find suitable representatives abroad;
- collect debts from foreign customers;
- employ specialist export staff.

The *facts,* however, are that:

- For selling to the European Union there is very little documentation to be completed additional to that necessary for domestic sales, and when exporting further afield your freight forwarder (see Chapter 9), export merchant (see Chapter 2), the Royal Mail Parcel Post service or, in certain circumstances, the foreign buyer, will handle the documentation on your behalf. And if you decide to 'do-it-yourself' from start to finish, you need only to learn the process once. You will not repeat any major mistakes made in the early stages.
- The DTI provides a wide range of free or low-cost services to help with market research (see Chapters 3 and 4), and many other inexpensive sources of information on foreign markets and business methods are readily available. A large amount of the basic research can be undertaken personally. This is not to say you will be able to avoid spending money later on when your research requirements become more refined, but you should at least be in a position to establish whether additional expenditures are likely to be worthwhile.
- Foreign agents and distributors can be located through British Embassies and Consulates via an extremely straightforward and inexpensive procedure (see Chapter 3).

- Extensive factoring services are available which result in your not having to worry about non-payment by foreign customers.
- Most of the detailed, nitty-gritty aspects of exporting can safely be left to outsiders, notably your bank, forwarder, insurance broker, credit factor and/or shipping agent, or foreign carrier. All aspects of exporting can be dealt with effectively, *provided* you are well-organised, reasonably knowledgeable about export methods, have a comprehensive export plan and genuine long-term commitment to foreign markets.

It is a myth, moreover, that only large firms can gain from exporting. Small businesses are flexible, benefit from faster decision making, can develop personal contacts with agents and customers, and are frequently highly successful when selling overseas. Indeed, export administration is often best completed when only a small number of people are involved.

Exporting is a multi-faceted activity not amenable to bureaucracy. If just one or two people deal with all aspects of an export order – personally handling the documentation, transport and payment arrangements, insurance, customs clearance, and so on – there is less likelihood of error. When mistakes do occur they may be rectified more easily. Also, the personal relationships established with foreign customers by the individuals who look after the firm's export function can be invaluable when seeking further export orders.

Need for a realistic approach

Irrespective of all the benefits potentially available from exporting it is vitally important not to be carried away by the apparent glamour of the process, and to make a cool assessment of all the problems likely to be associated with foreign sales. Note, in particular, that:

- because export customers are farther away than those in the UK it is not easy to 'troubleshoot' problems as they arise. Contractual terms assume greater importance for foreign than for UK sales and have to be followed *to the letter*;
- despite the availability of payments insurance and credit factoring, long delays can occur before export bills are finally settled, and insurance and factoring services themselves have a price;
- resolution of disputes with customers, foreign carriers, etc is likely to involve foreign laws and business practices;
- trading in foreign currencies creates the risk of exchange rate depreciation;

- although much of the detailed work associated with exporting can be contracted out to third parties, a certain amount of extra paperwork is bound to result. You are also still responsible for commissioning and co-ordinating outsiders' contributions;
- benefits from larger scale production (such as bulk purchasing of input components or the integration of processes) might not be available if national consumer tastes and other characteristics in various countries necessitate numerous product modifications. Note, moreover, that the costs of market entry (advertising and promotion, establishment of distribution networks, and so on) could themselves outweigh production savings.

The development of an export facility can place a severe strain on your business's resources, so great care must be taken when deciding whether or not to go ahead. Sound reasons for *not* actively exporting might include the following:

- The problem of acquiring and retaining staff with the linguistic and specialist foreign trade skills necessary for selling abroad.
- The inconvenience of having to find foreign agents and distributors and of investigating the market characteristics and trading rules of foreign countries.
- The cost of financing long periods between obtaining export orders, delivering the goods to distant destinations and getting paid.
- The managerial resources necessary to have people visit foreign markets regularly, monitor and control agents and distributors, meet important customers, attend foreign exhibitions, etc.
- Distance from foreign markets which can mean that some opportunities are missed, and that local competitors can easily respond to your export marketing campaigns.
- The fact that sales forecasting can be far more difficult for foreign countries than for the UK.

Further arguments against exporting could be that the resources needed to sell abroad might be more profitably employed in building up the home market and, importantly, that foreign sales could encourage a firm to delay introducing new products here in Britain and ignore the threat of domestic competition.

It is *essential* to realise that if a firm does not possess the resources to develop proper export facilities, but nevertheless attempts to do so 'on the cheap', the result can be an utter disaster. Living and operating within your own country enables you to obtain a 'feel' for the needs of the domestic market. Identification of unsatisfied demands in foreign countries takes money and time. Lack of these can result in half-baked export operations that are doomed to fail.

Is exporting for you?

Only you can decide whether exporting is really appropriate for your firm. But before committing yourself, remember that becoming involved in export *necessarily* means an expansion of the scope and nature of your business, so that the decision to get started needs to be taken just as seriously as any other decision to extend the scale of operations of the firm. Key questions to ask prior to starting up in export include the following:

- Is my product really likely to appeal to foreign customers? Your firm may be more fortunate in this respect than businesses based in a number of other countries: since Britain is a mature and sophisticated market, products which sell well here typically have a good chance of succeeding elsewhere in the world. Note, however, that it would be extremely foolish simply to *assume* that foreign customers will want to buy an item that is popular in the UK. Your product needs to have something special to make it attractive to foreign customers. Perhaps you can offer the item at a much lower price than local businesses, or have an exciting corporate image, or provide quality levels or customer care facilities not available from rival firms. Careful research is needed to identify possible success factors.
- Does the firm's management have the time and inclination to set up and administer an export function?
- Can you be reasonably sure that orders received from abroad will be delivered on schedule?
- How vulnerable is your business to cash flow problems possibly created by foreign customers' late payments?
- Is your firm's administrative system already overburdened? Exporting means more paperwork and correspondence (some of it in foreign languages). Much of this can be contracted out to specialist advisers, but the outsiders still have to be appraised and supervised. How will you cope with these extra duties?
- If you and/or your senior colleagues have to go abroad looking for business will the firm continue to operate efficiently while you are away?

- Do you have significant experience of modifying products to meet the requirements of different market sectors?
- Does the firm have ready access to short-term finance? Exporting is likely to create additional demands for working capital. Arranging suitable sources of finance can be a crucial export activity.

Taking the plunge

If you do decide to start exporting, it is vital that you remain fully committed to foreign sales. Avoid regarding exports as little more than a convenient means of shifting surplus output or you will end up having little to sell abroad in some periods but huge amounts at other times. The latter situation will result in your not being able to meet certain customers' orders and needing to warehouse large inventories of finished items awaiting export when domestic demand is slack!

Genuine commitment to exporting requires that you relate the export function to the firm's overall operations and regard *all* orders as having equal status, whether they originate at home or abroad. Export considerations must be taken into account when designing and developing products, when selecting transport and distribution systems, when dealing with banks, advertising agencies, and so on, and when structuring the overall organisation of the firm. You need to be willing to adapt your products for foreign markets and to spend money on researching the needs and characteristics of foreign customers. The firm must be prepared to handle foreign currency balances and to produce promotional materials in foreign languages.

The basic marketing tools that you use for domestic selling apply in general to exporting, although the problems encountered and the specific techniques needed to overcome them can differ considerably. You will need to alter the way you *think* about your marketing activities, which in your own country are undertaken in a familiar environment with known and accessible data sources and easy access to advertising media, market research firms and other providers of marketing services.

When exporting, however, circumstances and facilities vary among nations. Importantly, cultural, legal, political, economic and other environments differ between countries. Some consequences of this fact are discussed in Chapter 8.

Chapter 2
How to Export

Firms that export may do so passively or actively. *Passive* exporting occurs when a business receives orders from abroad without having canvassed them. *Active* exporting results from a firm developing policies for setting up systems for organising the export function and for dealing with export logistics, documentation and finance. This explains the use of the word 'active' in the titles of a number of government supported export assistance schemes.

The other crucial distinction is between *direct* exporting and *indirect* exporting. With indirect exporting you engage intermediaries to handle most (sometimes all) aspects of export deals. Returns are obviously lower than 'doing-it-yourself', but you are relieved of the need to deal with export administration, shipping, internal transport and so on, and you do not have to carry the risks of market failure. However, you lose control over final selling prices and how your products are presented, and foreign sales may fall because of poor foreign retailing and inadequate customer care.

The main intermediaries are (a) export houses, (b) confirming houses, and (c) UK-based offices of foreign firms (especially retail chains). Agents and distributors might also be regarded as 'intermediaries' in a certain sense, depending on circumstances and the nature of the agency or distribution contract. The roles and obligations of agents and distributors are discussed in Chapter 5.

Export houses

Export houses are firms that act as principals in export transactions, buying and selling on their own account. In effect, export houses (also known as export merchants) are wholesalers who buy goods in the supplying firm's country and resell them abroad, taking their profit from the difference in the prices at which they buy and sell. They operate in foreign markets through their own salespeople, stockists and, perhaps, retail outlets. Some specialise in particular countries, others in particular categories of goods. All have intimate knowledge of foreign markets. Dealing with an export merchant is essentially the same as selling to a domestic customer. Payment will be made on identical terms and conditions as in the UK.

An enormous benefit arising from the use of a well-established export house is that the client firm has immediate access to lists of large numbers of potential customers all over the world, saving the client a great deal of expensive foreign market research. Export houses themselves may possess extensive networks of agency contacts, distributorship arrangements and agreements with foreign banks, advertising agents and market research firms. Some large companies that normally undertake export activities in-house occasionally use export houses to sell in small and unfamiliar markets where it is not worth setting up sales arrangements independently.

Details of export houses operating in various countries and handling particular types of product are available from the British Exporters Association (BEA), which issues to its members a monthly list of exporting firms seeking assistance. You have to pay a small fee to be included in this list. Additionally, the BEA publishes a directory giving details of its members' interests, facilities and services.

Confirming houses

Confirming houses exist to represent, as principals, foreign buyers who are not sufficiently well known for home firms to supply them on credit terms. The confirming house finances the transaction and thus assumes the risk of customer default. In return, it charges the buyer a commission. The foreign customer sends you an order endorsed 'for confirmation and payment' by a named confirming house. The latter states on a separate document its willingness to accept responsibility for payment. As soon as the goods are ready for delivery you inform the confirming house, which arranges shipment and settles the supplier's invoice. Information on the activities of confirming houses – particularly when they have been instructed to look for suppliers of certain types of goods – can be obtained from the Export Intelligence Service of the DTI (see Chapter 3).

Buying offices

Major retailing groups, international organisations (the United Nations, for example) and purchasing agencies of national governments frequently maintain permanent 'buying offices' in the large industrial countries. They will purchase your output here in the UK and thereafter take care of all transport and foreign trade documentation. Chambers of Commerce and trade associations are among the best sources of information about the existence of buying offices in a particular field.

Also, there is an Export Buying Offices Association (EXBO), which is an organisation representing the London offices of leading overseas department stores and importers. Many UK consumer goods sold to foreign department stores are channelled through the Association's members, which can advise supplying firms on the suitability of their products for particular foreign markets. EXBO may only be contacted by fax, on 0171 351 9287. It issues a brochure outlining the main interests of its members.

Trade Research Publications publishes a *Directory of Export Buyers in the UK*, listing details of foreign buyers by product and country of destination. It also contains details of inward buying missions due to visit the UK. Addresses of local Chambers of Commerce can be obtained from the Association of British Chambers of Commerce. Contact points for trade associations appear in the *Directory of European Industrial and Trade Associations* published by CBD Research Ltd and in Euromonitor's *European Directory of Trade and Business Associations*. You should also approach your regional DTI office and ask whether it has any lists of buying offices that might be interested in the sorts of product you supply.

Direct exporting

Here, you do not bother with intermediaries, opting instead to assume complete personal control over transportation, customs clearance, internal distribution, local advertising, price policies and final sale. This work may be undertaken within an export department or through establishing a branch office in the foreign country. The latter option provides foreign customers with a local contact point with your firm and enhances the exported item's local image.

Should you use intermediaries?

For the novice exporter the use of intermediaries is almost essential. As you gain experience of export methods, however, you will need to decide whether your continuing involvement with intermediaries is financially worth while. Use of in-house facilities is perhaps most appropriate for a firm with a limited number of clearly identified foreign customers; where the costs of exporting are readily controlled;

and where minimal after-sales service is required. In-house support staff are obviously familiar with the business, its organisational structure and, importantly, they know exactly where to look for information. The people concerned are fully accountable for their actions and their careers substantially depend on the quality of their work. Yet doing things in-house has a number of disadvantages:

- The export department might become a 'little empire' devoted solely to the export function (regardless of the profitability of export sales).
- In-house staff are not subject to penetrating expert criticism from outside. Mistakes made by your own employees because of their lack of specialist skills and knowledge might never be revealed.
- Internal employees usually have limited experience of other industries and firms.
- Internal staff might be apathetic and lack the skills and innovative attitudes needed to complete an unusual or exceptionally difficult assignment on time.

Export houses, foreign wholesalers, buying consortia, etc may be more objective in their assessments of the probabilities of an exporter's products succeeding in foreign markets. Their extensive experience of the export problems of a wide range of firms and industries enables them to identify solutions quickly and to appreciate all the options available and the difficulties involved. Further advantages to using intermediaries include:

- not having to train and develop employees to perform a comparable role;
- savings on overheads (in-house export specialists might not be using their export skills for all of their working time);
- the fact that, in principle, intermediaries should possess up-to-the-minute knowledge of the latest exporting techniques and foreign market situations;
- possibly a higher level of motivation because intermediaries are driven by the need to make a profit through offering excellent services (rather than just earning an employee's salary). Also, they should have extensive contacts with other experts and export specialists in their particular field.

Choosing intermediaries
If you decide to use intermediaries extensively then (assuming you have a choice) prepare a shortlist and carefully examine each candi-

date firm's knowledge of your product and target foreign markets, experience and expertise, required margins, credit rating, customer care facilities and ability to promote your product in an effective way. Specific desirable characteristics of an intermediary might include:

- a solid financial base;
- a well-established corporate image in the local market;
- a good track record of selling similar items;
- wide geographical coverage;
- a substantial salesforce;
- warehousing facilities and a willingness to carry a significant amount of stock;
- procedures for prompt settlement of invoices.

Collaborative arrangements

Sometimes it is possible for small firms to form joint ventures (often under the auspices of a trade association) in order to market their collective outputs in foreign states. This spreads cost and means that ancillary services too expensive for a single firm can be arranged. The consortium might export under a separate corporate identity, negotiate bulk rates for transporting joint consignments, conduct international marketing research, draft uniform terms for contracts of sale, and arrange for the collection of debts.

Piggybacking

Another option is for a small business to seek a 'piggyback' deal with a large company which already operates in relevant foreign markets and is willing to act on behalf of other businesses. This enables larger companies to make full use of their sales representatives, premises, office equipment, etc in the countries concerned.

The carrier will purchase the goods outright or act as a commission agent, and may or may not sell the rider's product under the carrier's own brand name – depending on the details of the agreement.

A further option is to seek a 'sister company' in a foreign market. Sister companies are foreign firms which offer similar products and which will act as your foreign agent, advise on local conditions, translate documents, etc. In return, you provide reciprocal facilities to the other firm.

Chapter 3
Getting Help

A number of government schemes have been set up to help UK exporters. Access to some of these is free; others are chargeable, but very inexpensive. Government export assistance has been integrated under the name 'Overseas Trade Services' (OTS), which you will see on the promotional literature for certain programmes. OTS was formed by linking up the export-related activities of the Department of Trade and Industry and the Foreign and Commonwealth Office (via British Embassies, Consulates and other Diplomatic Posts in foreign countries) to provide a consolidated help and advisory service.

Normally, you access these facilities by telephoning your nearest DTI regional office whose number is in the telephone directory. Give the DTI as much information about your intentions as you can because a wide range of schemes is in operation. The main services and programmes on offer are as follows.

The Market Information Enquiry Service

This can be used once you have identified the need for detailed specialist information. It uses the services of UK Diplomatic Posts in foreign countries to answer UK exporters' *specific* questions relating to:

- local legislation;
- market prospects for particular products;
- characteristics of relevant local industries;
- economic information;
- the suitability of your product for a certain country;
- local competition;
- marketing methods appropriate for various markets;
- local responses to a test marketing exercise.

The service will also provide lists of local buyers, agents and distributors, but will not contact them. You pay a modest hourly fee, depending on the amount of work involved in assembling the information. Answers to queries normally (but not necessarily) arrive within four weeks. To access the scheme, contact your nearest DTI regional office which, free of charge, will provide examples of the types of information available.

The Export Market Intelligence Service

Each day the DTI's Export Intelligence Service (EIS) gathers, collates and distributes to UK exporters information obtained by the commercial sections of British Diplomatic Service Posts in foreign countries. Information provided includes overseas enquiries for various types of product, calls for tender, names and addresses of foreign agents wanting to represent British firms, background market information, etc.

To use EIS you have to subscribe direct or belong to a trade association or Chamber of Commerce that already has a subscription. Each subscriber submits a 'profile' to the system, itemising the types of information required (markets, products, etc). The EIS computer then matches its daily information inputs with these profiles and prints out the information relevant to each subscriber. This information is sent out by first-class post, fax or E-mail. Direct computer access is also available. You pay a small fee for each item of intelligence sent to your business.

The Export Marketing Research Scheme (EMRS)

EMRS is intended for firms that require a more structured approach to marketing research using the services of an outside adviser. The DTI will pay up to half the total cost of commissioning a consultant to undertake overseas market research, plus a third of the cost of purchasing published marketing research data. If you belong to a trade association which does or commissions research on your behalf, the DTI will pay up to 75 per cent of the cost. Expenditures incurred while researching technical standards requirements for certain types of equipment are also repayable.

The scheme offers free professional advice on how to set about conducting in-house research into foreign markets. Certain exceptions apply to the EMRS, namely:

- grant-assisted costs in excess of a certain threshold (which is higher for research conducted by a trade association – contact the DTI for details);
- costs of general directories and for updating subscriptions to journals;

- companies with more than 200 workers;
- firms that have already used the scheme more than three times;
- background research that is not part of a specific project;
- sales or promotional visits.

To use EMRS you need to approach the Association of British Chambers of Commerce (ABCC), which manages the scheme on behalf of the DTI.

The Export Representative Service

The DTI holds details of potential agents and/or distributors handling various types of product in all countries in which there are UK Diplomatic Posts. A shortlist of potential representatives whom you may contact direct can be produced at short notice or, if you prefer, the commercial department of the appropriate British Embassy or Consulate will undertake a detailed investigation of local firms most likely to be interested in acting on your behalf.

You need to supply the Embassy/Consulate with packages of your trade literature (brochures, price lists, credit terms, etc) plus sample products where appropriate. The more accurate the information provided the faster the response from relevant prospects. In the country in question a member of staff of the UK Embassy's commercial department will make direct contact with and normally visit prospective agents. The Embassy representative will show potential agents samples of your product and of (suitably translated) sales literature, and will make a record of their responses. The fee payable for the service depends on the number of hours' work involved.

Reports do not evaluate the creditworthiness of the agents, although credit checks can be obtained separately through the DTI's Overseas Status Report Service (see below). However, the report will detail listed agencies' interests, capacities, territories covered, warehousing facilities, after-sales service offered and other agencies held.

Overseas Status Report Service

This provides UK companies with information concerning the financial status and resources of foreign firms. The commercial department of the appropriate local British Diplomatic Post will report on a foreign business's trading activities, facilities, technical know-how, credit rating, and so on.

Reports take about four weeks to complete and are charged according to the number of hours that were necessary. Where the investigated firm is an agency, the report will list (where known) the other agencies it holds, its facilities, its capabilities, experience, etc. Note that the report will not offer an opinion regarding the foreign firm's creditworthiness; it will simply present as much relevant information as possible leaving you to make up your own mind.

The Programme Arranging Service (PAS)

This service can normally be activated within 12 months of your having used the Market Information Enquiry Service, Export Marketing Research Scheme or Export Representative Service. It is not available to firms that *already* have representation in the relevant foreign market. The DTI will arrange a programme of appointments and provide information on local etiquette and business practices, plus advice on local travel. You need to commission the service at least two months in advance of the intended visit. The service is chargeable. Fees depend on the number of hours' work necessary to complete the arrangements.

The In-Market Help Service (IMHS)

IMHS is another service available only as a follow-up to the Market Information Enquiry Service, Export Marketing Research Scheme or Export Representative Service and within 12 months of using one of these. As with PAS, the service is not available to firms that already have representation in a particular foreign market. A local expert will devise a programme of useful visits (for example, to potential agents), will accompany you on these visits, help you understand local culture and business methods, and give his or her impressions of the success of your discussions. The service cannot be used for 'political lobbying', debt collecting or the pursuit of legal actions. You have to book IMHS at least three months prior to the visit, and pay a fee according to the number of hours' work involved.

Technical Help for Exporters (THE)

This is a government subsidised programme, operated by the British Standards Institution, to assist exporters with problems relating to product design and technical standards. THE will advise on foreign safety and environmental requirements, certification practices, industry standards, etc. It will supply, translate and comment on foreign regulations, and assist in obtaining foreign approval for UK products.

Simple enquiries are answered free of charge over the telephone. For example, you might want to know the type of electric plug used in Mexico or the building regulations in Malaysia. Otherwise, the charge depends on the extent of the research needed to deal with the query. The likely scale of the charge will be advised in advance of the work commencing. On payment of an appropriate fee, a THE engineer will inspect your output to determine whether it meets relevant foreign technical standards and, if it does not, will specify the modifications necessary to ensure technical compliance. THE will also undertake detailed technical research (for which a government grant may be available) on your behalf.

THE carries a stock of over 500,000 foreign language and 10,000 English translations of foreign standards, regulations and Codes of Practice, and itself produces a wide range of guides, surveys and handbooks relating to foreign technical requirements. A list of these publications is available free of charge. For a small fee, it is possible for certain product categories to subscribe to a special updating service that will keep you up to date with changes in foreign technical standards in particular countries. All material supplied is in English and issued on a monthly basis.

Help with group trade missions

Each year, nearly 10,000 individuals join DTI-supported trade missions to foreign countries with financial help from OTS, usually to exhibit at foreign trade shows or in groups to assess markets 'in the field'. Accompanying a group mission to another country allows you to examine at first hand the market potential for your product, to meet possible representatives, observe local conditions and, importantly, to discuss common problems with more experienced exporters. The DTI offers financial assistance to approved trade associations, Chambers of Commerce or other non-profit making bodies arranging group field trips to foreign markets outside Western Europe. Two major schemes operate, as follows.

The Outward Mission Scheme
Groups need to be sponsored by a UK Chamber of Commerce, trade association or similar body, and travel together. The scheme is available for travel to any country outside Western Europe. Any size of business is eligible and may claim assistance for up to ten missions (though no more than five to Japan or three to any one other country).

The Trade Fairs Support Scheme
Financial assistance for exporters wishing to attend foreign exhibitions is available via the Fairs and Promotions Branch (FPB) of the

DTI. Each quarter the Branch publishes a list of the promotions it is prepared to support. Assistance is given to *groups* of British exporters attending an overseas fair, and covers 50 per cent of the following:

- The cost of hiring exhibition space.
- Design and construction of stands.
- Display materials.
- Access to a group interpreter.
- Publicity for exhibitors' products through the Central Office of Information.

Note that the cost of travel is only recoverable for a maximum of two persons to destinations *outside* Western Europe. Also, it is only possible to claim support for the first three exhibitions in a certain country (five for Japan or – subject to certain conditions – Germany and the USA). Three further conditions attach to the scheme:

- You have to arrive at the foreign destination at least a day before the exhibition opens in order to set up your stand.
- The stand must be properly staffed at all times.
- Travel arrangements, insurance and hotel bookings are your responsibility.

The DTI will remove from your shoulders the burden of booking space and having to deal with exhibition organisers, and provides on-site commercial officers to help overcome last-minute difficulties.

The European Union occasionally provides financial support for EU pavilions at selected international fairs as part of its External Market export promotion scheme. Activities (which could include background research studies and occasional trade missions) must appeal to industry across several EU states if they are to qualify for funding. The programme targets particular markets and is aimed at small to medium-sized EU enterprises. China, Korea and the United Arab Emirates are examples of countries in which EU financial export promotion events have taken place. For further information contact the Commission of the European Communities DG 1A3 (address on page 182).

The Trade Fair Pamphleting Scheme (TFPS)

The DTI will help UK firms that are unable physically to attend certain important trade fairs and exhibitions to establish a presence via the Trade Fair Pamphleting Scheme, which offers exporters the opportunity to display their pamphlets, catalogues, brochures, etc on a group stand usually organised by a Chamber of Commerce or trade association. The service can only be used once per country, and companies must not have previously exhibited at the event in question. It is only available for literature on products manufactured in, or services provided from, the UK.

The DTI will need to satisfy itself that the exporting firm is capable of meeting the foreign demand likely to arise from the promotion, and charges fees that vary from exhibition to exhibition. Staff looking after the group stand collect lists of contacts who have expressed an interest in receiving further details of participating companies' products (including potential agents and distributors). 'Red hot' leads are notified to participants immediately by fax or telephone. Otherwise contacts are passed on within 30 days of the event, together with a written report on the level of interest shown in the product.

OTS commercial publicity services

These are currently available for 80 countries and designed to help groups of exporters use the foreign press for promotional purposes and reach overseas customers direct. Some of the services are free; others are chargeable but heavily subsidised. Assistance is co-ordinated by OTS and operates as follows.

1. OTS approaches the UK Central Office of Information which then contacts the group's sponsors and relevant Diplomatic Commercial Posts overseas in order to determine the nature and extent of the publicity support required.
2. A 'curtain-raiser' press release outlining each participating business's products is prepared and distributed free of charge to the local foreign press up to three months before the trade mission's arrival.
3. An exhibition or mission news statement is composed (for a small fee) detailing the particularly newsworthy aspects of the products of individual firms, which for an additional fee can have a 'company write-up' drafted and sent to the business editors of local newspapers. Also the (chargeable) 'New Products from Britain Service' (see below) is available to specific companies.
4. A 'Made in Britain' A4 illustrated promotional leaflet carrying up to 500 words and a photograph can be printed for each participating business, in multiples of 1,000 copies. These may be handed out at exhibitions or used in direct mail campaigns. Also

an illustrated group brochure can be produced at 50 per cent cost.

5. If appropriate, an eight-page advertising supplement showing the group's products and services may be prepared and inserted in a relevant local trade magazine, again at half the actual cost.

For full details of the above contact your DTI regional office.

Overseas stores promotions

The Fairs and Promotions Branch will also provide financial help to major foreign retail outlets wishing to mount in-store promotions of UK goods. The DTI advises British firms on how to participate effectively in such a promotion and informs buying offices in the local market of the event. News about forthcoming in-store promotions is distributed by the FPB.

Overseas seminars

If a Chamber of Commerce or trade association arranges a seminar aimed at bringing together influential people capable of stimulating the overseas sales of its members' products, the DTI will meet 45 per cent of the following costs:

- hire of an auditorium plus supporting services;
- translation and printing of papers;
- local publicity;
- the fee of one internationally known speaker;
- hiring local staff;
- hospitality;
- display material;
- use of interpreters.

The DTI is also prepared to offer Chambers of Commerce and trade associations low-cost help with the actual organisation of seminars in foreign countries. Subject to resource availability, UK foreign Diplomatic Posts will arrange a package of support for an event, including the booking of conference rooms and facilities, identification of possible invitees, provision of advice on local business practices, and general troubleshooting and administration of the seminar. The cost depends on the number of hours' work required.

Inward missions

The DTI will provide financial assistance to trade associations or Chambers of Commerce that invite foreigners who are capable of influencing the purchase of UK goods to visit Britain. The 'Inward Mission' scheme, as it is called, will advise on organisational aspects of the visit and will pay:

- 50 per cent of foreign visitors' travel costs, including relevant travel within the UK;
- 50 per cent of interpreting fees;
- visitors' accommodation and meals (up to a certain threshold);
- half the costs of a reception, lunch or dinner for briefing or debriefing foreign guests.

For further information contact the DTI's Fairs and Promotions Branch.

The New Products from Britain Service

This is intended to generate foreign interest in British firms' products by encouraging overseas magazines and journals to publish feature articles on new British products as they are launched in local markets.

A press release describing your product is written by a professional journalist and then translated and targeted at suitable foreign publications. All you have to do is provide the UK Central Office of Information (which organises the scheme) with brochures and other publicity materials, and to respond to telephone calls if further information is required. The product must be newsworthy in order to attract foreign attention. A small fee is payable, which covers up to 15 selected target markets. Press releases are normally available to local British Diplomatic Posts within eight weeks of a decision to use the service.

Export Development Advisers

In conjunction with Chambers of Commerce, the DTI has set up a network of Export Development Advisers, each of whom is an experienced exporter able to offer specialist advice on all stages of the export process. Contact your nearest DTI regional office for details of the scheme.

Business in Europe

DTI assistance for selling in Western Europe has been consolidated under the 'Business in Europe' scheme which offers a wide range of services, including all those previously outlined as they apply to the EU. To find out about these services, telephone the DTI's Business in Europe Hotline on 01272 444 888.

Euro information centres

The European Commission has established a number of *Centres for European Business Information* in all EU countries These exist to provide businesses with data and limited advice on EU activities, including: EU grants and other sources of financial assistance; new EU legislation and updates on product standardisation. Centres are not consultancy organisations *per se*, but should be able to direct enquiring firms towards further sources of help and information. You can obtain the address of your nearest Centre from the DTI's European 'All Country Desk' or from a DTI regional or satellite office. Centres hold all official EU documents, including the *Official Journal*, which contains full details of every major public sector contract made available for tender within the European Union. Centres also hold EU-sponsored industry/sector studies, which frequently contain valuable information for exporters.

Other sources of assistance

Trade associations and Chambers of Commerce are obviously useful for obtaining information and advice, as are high street banks. HM Customs and Excise has set up a network of advice centres to provide information to businesses on customs matters.

There are around 70 Export Clubs located in various parts of the country. Members meet to discuss solutions to common problems, pool ideas, share practical knowledge and learn from each others' experiences. Clubs are directly supported by the DTI, and operate under the aegis of local Chambers of Commerce, Training and Enterprise Councils or trade associations. Further information may be obtained from the Export Clubs Advisory Committee (ECAC) or from the DTI.

Chapter 4

Organising for Export and Doing Research

The main decisions you will have to take once you begin exporting are:

- whether to handle delivery and documentation yourself or leave this to outsiders (such as a freight forwarder);
- the delivery and payments terms and currency to quote;
- the extent of the insurance cover to take out;
- whether to protect yourself against possible adverse currency movements;
- how to finance export transactions;
- the best means for advertising and otherwise promoting your output in foreign markets.

Even if you make extensive use of intermediaries, someone within your firm will have to assume responsibility for co-ordinating their activities, and it is likely that, as your experience of exporting increases, you will wish to do more and more of the practical work yourself (thereby removing intermediaries' mark-ups and commissions and significantly reducing total export costs). Firms with substantial volumes of exports require export departments to initiate, oversee and co-ordinate export duties.

Note, however, that it is possible to subcontract your entire export function to a specialist who will simultaneously handle the export work of several client companies, 'lock, stock and barrel'. Your goods will be exported under your own name, but you have no administrative overheads relating to exporting and need not recruit and develop dedicated export employees. Through managing the exports of a number of firms at the same time the outsider might secure cost economies that can be passed back to clients via lower fees, especially if he or she specialises in a limited range of complementary products.

Another possible advantage to using an export management company is that since it will be paid on a commission basis, it should be highly motivated to increase your foreign sales. However, there are problems associated with this approach. The outsider might become overextended through taking on the work of too many clients and may not possess the intimate knowledge of foreign markets and product categories that he or she alleges. Also note that by using this type of facility you abandon all possibilities for acquiring export know-how within your own firm. If you are interested in using an export management company, contact the Institute of Export, which might be able to provide a list of firms engaged in this line of activity in your region, and look in *Yellow Pages* under the headings 'Export managers' and 'Export consultants'.

Setting up an export department

Export activities cannot be completed successfully on a piecemeal basis by individuals who are predominantly engaged in other tasks: there are so many specialist jobs, documents and procedures to be dealt with that it is essential to have at least one person clearly responsible for the total export process from beginning to end. Hence, if you do not already employ people with appropriate backgrounds, you will need to recruit or train specialist staff competent in the techniques of foreign trade, the financing of export transactions and in shipping and other transport documentation. These people must be knowledgeable about various world markets and will probably be multilingual (though note the impossibility of anyone being able to speak the languages of all the countries with which you might do business).

The work of the export section must be taken seriously by everyone in the firm and the export manager involved in all relevant functions: market research, negotiation of agency and distribution contracts, product development and modification for foreign markets, liaison with foreign advertising media, transport, arranging the clearance of letters of credit, packaging, and the organisation of after-sales service in foreign countries. Also, the export manager needs to have a say in overall business planning, decisions concerning the design and development of new products, liaison with banks and advertising agencies, sales forecasting, the recruitment and training of marketing personnel, and the control of salespeople 'in the field' while they are on foreign assignments.

It is in the nature of export work that the section completing it will be more self-contained than other departments. This sometimes results in export departments becoming too embroiled in the nitty-gritty of export techniques and procedures and pursuing their own objectives at the expense of those of the wider business. A common problem with having a self-contained export department is that foreign sales increase substantially, but without any attempt to enlarge and reconstitute the department, resulting in its staff assuming ever-widening responsibilities for which they are not properly prepared or resourced.

Handling export salespeople

Good export salespeople are not like other mortals, so before you hire any you need to know *exactly* how they operate and what you can do to help them succeed. Visits to customers by salespeople 'in the field' are extremely valuable. They establish a social relationship between the firm and its customers, enable the local market testing of products, and can be used to resolve amicably problems with agents and distributors and to settle customer complaints. Sending representatives to foreign countries is expensive, but still far cheaper than setting up branch offices in other nations, especially when the total value of orders is likely to be small. Because of the high cost of using travelling salespeople it is *essential* that they return with orders, so great care in the selection and control of export salespeople has to be applied.

Like all effective representatives, export salespeople must be personable, persuasive and able quickly to identify and understand customer demands. Over and above these qualities, however, the export salesperson must be competent to conduct on-the-spot market research (including the investigation of competitors' activities), and a high degree of responsibility has to be assumed. Export salespeople negotiate with customers and take significant decisions; they represent to foreign customers the management of your firm and cannot be seen constantly referring to head office for instructions. The individual has to be able to answer queries face to face regarding, for example, technical servicing, transport arrangements and schedules, penalty clauses, contract details and the options available for financing the deal.

Export salespeople normally deal with very senior managers in client organisations. Hence, they need to be able to weigh up situations, assess risk, evaluate options on the basis of limited information and take important decisions without consultative support.

As well as possessing linguistic skills, an export salesperson must have the patience to cope with long periods spent travelling abroad (and all problems and frustrations attached thereto: lost luggage, incorrect hotel reservations, etc), a cool temperament and the ability to cope with stress. He or she must be able rapidly to acclimatise to local cultures, customs and business practices. A flight from, say, the Middle East to Scandinavia takes only a few hours, yet the differences in approach to business in the two locations are worlds apart.

An export salesperson's work regularly takes him or her into unfamiliar environments within which he or she must operate alone and without supervision. Hence, the individual needs to be a mature, stable and dependable person who genuinely enjoys foreign travel and can be relied upon not to waste time in remote foreign locations.

When selecting people to undertake this role, look for characters who are neutral on political and social issues, diplomatic, likely to be sensitive to local cultures and have genuinely international perspectives – able to forget that they are nationals of a particular state.

Candidates must be knowledgeable about foreign business cultures or know where to look up this information. Business cultures differ across a wide range of matters: punctuality; modes of dress for and conduct during business meetings; whether the use of handshakes and first names are appropriate; conventions concerning the discussion of business over lunch; the role of humour during conversations, and many other details.

Support your export salespeople by:

- providing first-class promotional literature. Remember that potential foreign customers will probably never have heard of your business and are not able easily to carry out checks on the integrity of your firm. Customers want to see some concrete and visible evidence of the supplying company's ability to deliver on time at an appropriate level of quality and to provide prompt and efficient after-sales service. Foreign buyers frequently assume that problems can be sorted out more quickly and easily with local businesses than with an enterprise in another country;

- keeping foreign visits as short as possible. Social isolation can be a serious problem for a travelling export salesperson. Personal relationships with colleagues and customers during a trip will usually be of a strictly formal business nature, leading perhaps to loneliness, boredom and the collapse of personal motivation. During a field trip the salesperson is constantly on duty, meaning perhaps that he or she is working 14 hours per day during the week, and travelling, checking in and out of hotels, etc at weekends! Business might have to be conducted in the evenings;

reports to head office have to be written; plans for the next leg of the trip drafted, and so on.

Researching foreign markets

The sorts of information you need to gather on potential foreign markets include:

- whether there is a significant demand for your type of product and, if so, how quickly demand is growing. This requires analysing trends in sales in various countries. Always use local currency values in real terms (that is, having been adjusted for the effects of local inflation) for this measure rather than sterling or US dollar estimates: fluctuations in currency exchange rates can cause dramatic swings in reported sales figures quoted in sterling and dollar terms, even though local currency values are unaltered. You need figures on sales of the relevant product category by region, customer type and (if available) selling methods;
- average order size and customer spend;
- the composition of the buying public;
- demographic information, such as the age structure of the population, religious groupings, the number of households and average household size, social conditions, regional distribution of the population and its rate of expansion;
- inflation and unemployment rates, trends in gross domestic product, local business confidence indicators, etc;
- consumer characteristics in terms of cultural attitudes (marriage and divorce rates, for example), educational levels, living standards, average income and income distribution;
- spending patterns in relation to percentages of consumer purchases made in supermarkets, hypermarkets, independent retailers and department stores;
- tastes, lifestyles and spending patterns of customers in particular foreign markets;
- nature of local distribution channels, especially the number and calibre of retail outlets;
- tariff levels and import restrictions (exchange controls, for example);
- special technical standards that have to be met within the market;
- costs and availability of credit and cargo insurance;
- local norms regarding credit periods and terms of payment;

- the degree of risk attached to doing business in the market;
- the maximum prices you will be able to charge.

Obtaining information on some of the above might seem a tall order at first sight, but you will be surprised how much data is available on advanced industrial countries, especially the USA and Western Europe. However, research into Third World markets is extremely difficult and the figures eventually obtained very unreliable. There are few published statistics and a general absence of local research companies able to gather accurate information. (The small average size of enterprise common in Third World countries means there are few local businesses with the resources necessary to buy significant amounts of marketing research.)

Initially, you might want to use a specialist market research firm to investigate candidate markets. These can be based here in the UK or in the country you wish to research. UK-based research companies are usually preferable for the novice exporter as they offer 'one-stop shopping' (a large research company should be capable of supplying all your research needs) and have wide-ranging experience of similar assignments already completed for other businesses. Hence, you benefit indirectly from other exporting companies' research efforts.

When choosing a UK-based firm you can conveniently invite proposals from several businesses, compare their costs, personally discuss your requirements with each candidate and examine examples of past assignments completed for other clients. Also, you can quickly evaluate the quality of the research firm's contributions.

But take care. A UK firm might not itself be competent to investigate a particular foreign market and, if it simply subcontracts to locally based foreign research firms, you not only lose control over the work but also have to pay margins to two research companies! You also have no easy means for establishing whether the local subcontractor is performing satisfactorily. It might be cheaper and more efficient to hire a foreign research firm directly. A local business is close (culturally as well as geographically) to local consumers and should be able to assess local consumer attitudes and tastes quickly and accurately.

Analysis of competitors
Considering the high costs of international marketing research and the uncertainties involved it is not surprising that many businesses choose not to commit extensive resources to this activity, relying instead on intuitive judgements and close observation of the activities

of local competing firms in the foreign market. Bad decisions resulting from faulty research data can actually *reduce* the profitability of selling abroad. Competitor analysis can be highly cost effective and should cover the following:

- Details of the strengths and weaknesses of competitors' products and how these compare with the outputs of your own firm. This information is available from competitors' brochures, leaflets and other promotional literature and/or through purchasing their products.
- *Why* competitors choose to operate in particular markets. Note how the absence of competition in a particular market could indicate an inhospitable environment, possibly including negative government attitudes towards foreign companies. Lists of competitors' distributors are usually given out freely in response to customer enquiries. Also, competitors' advertisements often specify where and how their product may be purchased.
- Competitors' terms of sale and the credit periods they offer.
- The financial performances of competing firms. It is easier to obtain this information for limited companies (which must publish their accounts) than for other types of business. Trade magazines frequently publish market surveys with analyses of the major businesses in particular markets. Such articles present estimates of the total extents of markets, the market shares of various firms, competitors' histories, profitabilities, selling and distribution methods and advertising style.
- The themes and concepts used in competitors' promotional materials. This requires putting together a folio of each competitor's advertisements.
- Prices and pricing history of competitors' brands, particularly the environmental changes that caused alterations in pricing strategies.
- The timing and seasonality of competitors' campaigns, and the implication of these timings for how competitors perceive their target audiences.

Desk research

Information for in-house desk research is available from:

- publications of national statistical offices. All countries have state statistical services that collect data, conduct surveys and publish the results. Increasingly, this information is available on

CD-ROM and may be accessed via cross-border packet switching systems. Major libraries such as the Science Reference Library and City Business Library in London offer chargeable database search facilities, and there are firms, known as 'information brokers', that specialise in this task. A list of information brokers operating in EU countries is available free of charge via the EU's ECHO database *Brokersguide*, which is updated monthly. Further details can be obtained from ECHO in Luxembourg.

- directories and data books issued by private publishing companies (Euromonitor's *International Data and Statistics*, for example);
- databases held by database hosts such as DIALOG or FT PROFILE;
- statistics gathered by international organisations, notably the OECD, United Nations, European Commission and the International Monetary Fund;
- Chambers of Commerce and trade associations;
- market research reports published by market research companies;
- trade and technical magazines;
- the DTI's Export Market Information Centre, which is based in London and holds worldwide statistics on patterns of trade and the main imports and exports of various nations, information on particular countries and products, and a selection of market research reports. The Centre also has an extensive collection of foreign mail-order catalogues, economic development plans for specific countries plus chargeable, online database search facilities. It is advisable to telephone or fax the Centre prior to a visit in order to establish that the information you require is available.

The quality of secondary information can vary enormously from nation to nation. Generally, the lower the per capita GDP within a country the more difficult it is to research.

HS numbers

Trade information on products is classified in most countries under Harmonised Commodity Description and Coding System (HS) numbers, which must be quoted in customs documentation when items are exported or imported.

The HS system is used worldwide for tariff categorisation, customs valuations and the compilation of import and export statistics. It has 21 main industry sections with numerous subdivisions, generating a ten-digit code for a specific product. You will need the relevant HS number in order to research several critical variables pertaining to your product. The numbers themselves are shown in the *Tariff Register,* published by HM Customs and available in some (but not all) public libraries. Otherwise, you will have to ask HM Customs and Excise for the appropriate HS numbers for your products. For countries which use different systems, published tables convert local classifications into HS numbers. A special, easy-to-use version of the HS system is used within the EU and is known as TARIC.

Once you know the relevant HS number you can use the DTI's tariffs, regulations and licences service that provides information on tariffs, local taxes and exchange controls applicable to particular foreign markets.

Field trips

Do *not* visit a foreign market until you have conducted a thorough examination of facts and figures about it here in the UK. Within Britain you can find an abundance of published materials on markets abroad, many of them available in public libraries. There is no point in travelling to another country simply to collect information that can be obtained at home: time spent on market research during a foreign trip might be better devoted to other things (for example, face-to-face contact with possible agents).

Reasons for visiting a potential market

Without doubt, contacts established during visits to a foreign market greatly improve an exporter's chance of success. A field trip enables you to investigate markets, to speak personally to local people (agents, consular officials, media representatives, etc) who can help you to sell the goods, and generally get the feel of local business conditions. Most importantly, you can assess the extent of local competition at first hand. Details of public holidays, customary business hours, local etiquette, etc for various countries are contained in booklets, *Hints for Exporters* available (at modest cost) from the DTI. A planned itinerary is essential. Arm yourself with a long list of *specific* questions to be answered during the visit, and the names and addresses of people you need to see. The DTI will help you to organise the trip, for which financial assistance may be available.

Chapter 5
Finding Customers

A difficult problem is deciding which countries to target for your export campaigns. In principle, every country in the world is a candidate for market entry, so it is necessary to have a system for reducing the list of possibilities to manageable dimensions.

Prospecting for foreign customers is akin to exploring for geological mineral deposits. You might not be able physically to observe their presence in a particular area, but the probabilities of their actually being there can be estimated from the characteristics of the *environments* in which they might be found. The existence and strength of certain key indicators in particular markets should signify the likelihood of there being significant numbers of potential customers in that area.

Unfortunately, searching for information on numerous foreign countries can be a colossal task that could easily crowd out other important activities. Thus, a logical, disciplined and structured approach to market selection needs to be applied.

Begin your search by defining as carefully as you can the types and characteristics of the foreign customers most likely to buy your product, and then look for countries that might contain large numbers of people satisfying these criteria. Next, make a list of the countries in which it will be easiest to sell your output, for example, because you or some of your managerial colleagues speak the language, or because you are familiar with the business methods used in the country, or because minimal modification of your product or the way you present it will be required.

The aim is to eliminate as quickly as possible all markets offering little chance of success (in view of the high cost of conducting research) while not improperly knocking out candidate countries with genuine potential. Some of today's poorer countries will be tomorrow's most dynamic markets, and the speed of transition is increasing. For example, Turkey and Brazil doubled their per capita GDPs over 20-year periods in the 1950s and 1960s. South Korea and China achieved this feat in ten years (the former from 1966, the latter from 1978), and current growth rates in certain parts of the world will reduce the necessary period yet again.

Selection criteria

Initially, you will have to gather information of a general nature on each foreign market that might be a candidate for entry. The range of available data is very broad and needs to be categorised in an appropriate manner. Hence, you must concentrate on those aspects of each country that are *particularly* relevant for the success of your product.

Examples of significant variables might include (depending on the nature of the item):

- proportion of the population within specific age and income groups;
- the size and buoyancy of the market, its rate of growth and trends in the demand for your product;
- the nature and extent of local competition;
- ease of doing business in the country, including distribution systems. A popular approach to selecting countries is to go for those with which the managers of the exporting firm are most familiar, such as through having visited them on holiday, being able to speak the language, or which are known to have low import tariffs and/or business environments and systems similar to those of the UK. However, bear in mind that the most lucrative markets for a particular type of product may in fact be found elsewhere – in countries that do not immediately spring to mind and where trading within the market is perhaps more problematic;
- the availability of export credit insurance or factoring services (see Chapter 12) for trade with that nation;
- economic and political stability;
- whether local technical product standards will require your adapting the specification of your product;
- ratio of urban to rural dwellers (essential information for the marketing of consumer durables in poorer countries);
- average age of dwellings by region and average family size;
- literacy rates and schooling periods;
- tariff and non-tariff entry barriers, foreign exchange controls on importers, the structure and rate of growth of imports by value and product.

More general considerations are population size and rate of expansion, lifestyles, promotional costs, debt-collecting facilities, legal controls on trade, and government attitudes towards business. You will have to use your own initiative to prepare a list of factors particularly relevant to the items you wish to export, although market size and population characteristics are two variables that are almost certain to be prominent.

Market size and spending power

The first things to look at under this heading are: the country's Gross Domestic Product in total and per head of population (noting the great disparities of income and wealth that exist within many countries); private consumption spending; and rates of ownership of motor cars and consumer durables. If most residents of a nation have incomes near the national average then their purchasing habits are likely to be similar. Typically, however, very many people are far below the average, indicating large differences in living standards with a few consumers being extremely rich and the majority poor. An even distribution of income and wealth is desirable for marketing consumer durables and other middle-income products; uneven distribution might help sales of extremely expensive, superluxury items. Another relevant factor is the country's rate of inflation, which determines real (as opposed to nominal) changes in standards of living.

It may be possible to identify countries at the same level of economic development and with consumers who exhibit the same patterns of demand. For countries at similar levels of economic development as the UK it might be useful to find the variables with which demand for your product is most closely correlated here in Britain, and then look for these variables in other nations.

The degree of urbanisation of the population may be a relevant factor in assessing spending power. City dwellers tend to be richer and better educated than people who live in remote rural areas. They are easier to reach and more likely to respond positively to advertising, and the communications, transport and warehousing systems of urban areas are more advanced. Urbanites are usually more cosmopolitan in outlook than their rural compatriates. Note also the high illiteracy rates in many nations with large numbers of rural dwellers.

Further indicators of market size include:

- levels of domestic production and imports to the market of the item in question;
- number of firms serving the market;

- level of exports of the product from the foreign country (if this is high it might suggest limited demand for the item within the market);
- rate of increase of the local price of the product relative to the local rate of inflation (a large differential implies a heavy demand for the item).

Population characteristics

In general, the bigger a country's population the better since, other things being equal, more potential customers can be approached (although in many cases a large part of the population might not be remotely interested in buying a particular type of goods, or may not have the money to do so). Other important considerations are the age structure of the population and its rate of expansion. Different age groups have disparate needs, incomes, perspectives and buying habits, so the age structure of the population could be crucial for products that appeal to particular age categories.

The geographical area over which the population is distributed might also be important. The lower the population density per square kilometre the more difficult and expensive it is to distribute goods. High population growth is a double-edged sword from the exporter's point of view; it creates more consumers but may at the same time reduce average living standards and per capita GDP. It is a fact that the poorest countries have the highest rates of population expansion.

Market selection: a summary of procedures

Here is a summary of the procedures you might adopt in order to select the countries on which to concentrate your export efforts.

1. Identify any special aspects of your product that render it unsuitable for sale in particular countries, for example, religious or cultural taboos or climatic conditions that make storage or use of the item impossible.
2. Determine the extent of your financial commitment to exporting (as discussed in Chapters 1 to 3) and assess the constraints this imposes on your choice of market. For example, are you prepared to hire specialist export staff and/or people who are fluent in particular foreign languages? Can you afford to offer warranties, after-sales service, etc demanded in some foreign countries but not required here in the UK? If your commitment is modest, you

will be looking for markets with well-developed and easily accessible ancillary business services (advertising agencies, agents, market research firms, etc) to help with export marketing tasks.

3. Pinpoint the key market characteristics especially relevant to selling your product, such as age distribution of the population, rates of ownership of consumer goods. Collect data on appropriate variables.

4. Look at tariff levels in each candidate country, possible selling prices and net profit margins.

5. Establish the availability and costs of payments insurance and/or factoring services in target nations.

6. Assess the ease of distribution within each possible market: retailing systems, availability of intermediaries, etc.

7. Examine the extent and nature of competition in various markets, and whether existing local firms might be able to prevent you selling your goods (via their control of distributors, for instance).

8. Assess the promotional opportunities available in each country. Are local advertising media suitable for your product? How much will advertising cost? How much extra promotion over and above that undertaken by local competing firms will you have to complete in order to gain a foothold in the market?

9. Prepare a shortlist of candidate markets. Do an intensive search for yet further information on these countries, taking outside advice where appropriate.

Sources of information for market screening

A useful starting point when searching for possible foreign markets is the publication *British Exports* (Kompass) which lists the major products in each product category and the overseas areas they serve. You can quickly establish the main markets to which existing exporters are currently sending particular types of goods. If you advertise in the *British Exports* directory, your details will also appear on-line through BT's Telecom Gold, Dialog and Istel databases, which can reach potential buyers worldwide.

Europ Production (ABC-Verlagshaus) is another useful publication. It is a multilingual register of European exports arranged by product, industry, company and country. For those who feel comfortable delving into government statistics, a general overview of which UK products are being sold in large quantity in which foreign markets is contained in a monthly HMSO publication, *Overseas Trade Statistics of the United Kingdom*, which you could have a quick look at in order to establish the main countries where products like yours are most likely to succeed. The extent of other nations' exports of these products to these countries can be ascertained from the *Statistics of Foreign Trade*, published by OECD. Only the largest public libraries stock these documents, but all libraries belong to networks that can direct you to where they can be found.

It is important to identify major consortium buyers (addresses of purchasing offices of chains of department stores, for example) of your types of product in target countries. The DTI can usually tell you where to locate such lists. Additionally, *Kompass* directories, to be found in most main libraries, can be invaluable here. There are *Kompass* directories of firms and products for most developed countries. Dun and Bradstreet also publish directories of companies in many states.

It may also be worthwhile looking at some of the guides to 'Doing Business in . . .' various countries published by the accounting firm Price Waterhouse. The looseleaf *Croner's Reference Book for Exporters* (Croner Publications) has brief details of the import regulations and trade and exchange control restrictions of virtually all countries in the world.

Potential corporate buyers in Continental Europe

A wealth of published and on-line sources is available for researching potential purchasing companies in Western Europe. Major on-line services include *European Kompass On-line*, which has information on the directors, products and numbers of employees of more than 300,000 companies in 12 countries, *International Dun's Market Identifiers* (Dun and Bradstreet), and *Financial Times Company Abstracts*. The last two are available via Dialog.

Reuters has a *Dataline* database containing details of about 3,000 leading European companies, as does CCN Business Information Ltd. *Predicasts Europe* contains information on companies, products and markets taken from 2,000 international trade and business publications.

Important hard copy sources of company information include:

- Dun and Bradstreet's *Principal International Businesses* and *Who Owns Whom: Continental Europe*; the latter is an annual, two-volume listing of around 8,000 parent companies and 90,000 of their subsidiaries in European states.
- ABC Europ Production's *The Universal Register of European Exporters*, a multilingual register of European exporters arranged by product, industry, company and country.

- Graham and Trotman's *Major Companies of Europe*, an annual, three-volume directory of 8,000 European firms; and *Medium Companies of Europe*.
- ELC International's *Europe's 15,000 Largest Companies*.
- *Europages*, a directory of companies in 24 European countries, available in English and several other languages.
- Reed Information Services' *Contact Europe*, which gives very basic details for around 400,000 European industrial businesses.

European retail outlets

The monthly subscription service *Retail Monitor International* (Euromonitor) gives extensive data and reports on trends in international retailing. Euromonitor also publish *Retail Trade International* which details facts and figures on retail markets, outlets and consumer expenditure in 19 countries, and the *European Directory of Retailers and Wholesalers*, covering around 3,000 European distribution companies and including details of their turnovers, buyers and product specialisations.

Other useful hard copy sources of information on European retailers include *Store Buyer International* (Manor House Press) which has the names of about 9,000 buyers in Europe's main stores; and Newman Books' *Directory of European Retailers*, an annual publication with data on the floor spaces, directors, buyers, etc of around 4,000 large, European retailing organisations.

Use of agents and distributors

Once you have determined the countries in which you intend doing business the next step will be to appoint local agents and distributors to handle your goods. However, there is no immutable law compelling you to use a local representative. You may wish to deal with customers direct and to arrange your own warehousing, distribution and customer care services. Much depends on the precise nature of your business, how much time you and your colleagues have to devote to export matters, and the extent to which your existing sales literature needs to be adapted (apart from the obvious question of translation to suit foreign requirements).

Agents and distributors

The difference between an agent and a distributor is that whereas a distributor actually *purchases* your products (thereby assuming full responsibility for their condition, sale and any bad debts), an agent simply puts you in touch with third parties but then 'drops out' of resulting contracts, so that the agreements are solely between you and the third parties. An agent will find foreign customers for your products under your or its own name (normally the former), but if the goods are defective, damaged or delivered late, it is you and not the agent who is responsible. It is also you, not the agent, who must assume responsibility for insurance, customs clearance, etc.

Agents operate on a commission basis. A *del credere* agent is one who, in return for a higher commission, indemnifies the supplying firm against the customers' bad debts. Agents may or may not hold stocks of your goods. If they do carry inventory, they are sometimes called 'distribution agents'. This type of agent is useful for products that might be required at short notice, which sell better in showroom surroundings, and/or are normally sold after customer examination and in small quantities.

Distributors typically demand exclusivity. Note how exclusivity clauses in a distribution agreement can create legal difficulties because exclusive trading arrangements are not generally permitted under the competition laws of most industrialised nations. Even if no exclusivity arrangement is specified, a distributor will almost certainly insist on receiving more favourable terms than other purchasers, again causing legal problems.

In the European Union, geographically exclusive distribution agreements are exempt from competition law provided (a) there exist alternative sources of supply of that type of product in the area covered, and (b) customers in the distributor's territory are free to obtain the goods from at least one other source apart from the exclusive distributor. The latter source can be a distributor in an adjacent territory or direct supply from the supplier's own premises. Also, at least one of the parties must have a turnover less than (currently) 100 million ECUs per annum.

Agency law
Certain general principles apply to the law of agency in all nations, namely that:

- an agent cannot take delivery of the principal's goods at an agreed price and resell them for a higher amount without the principal's knowledge and permission;
- agents must maintain strict confidentiality regarding their principals' affairs and must pass on all relevant information;

- the principal is liable for damages to third parties for wrongs committed by an agent 'in the course of his or her authority', for example, if the agent fraudulently misrepresents the principal's firm.

Thereafter, however, agency law differs markedly between nations, especially in relation to agents' rights on termination of their contracts. The European Union situation has been largely reconciled by a Directive on Agency effective in all EU nations since 1994. Under the Directive, an agent whose agreement is terminated is entitled to (a) full payment for any deal resulting from his or her work (even if it was concluded *after* the end of the agency), (b) compensation (where appropriate) for damages to the agent's commercial reputation caused by an unwarranted termination. Outside Western Europe, some countries regard agents as basically *employees* of client organisations; others see agents as self-contained and independent businesses. It is essential to ascertain the legal position of agency agreements in each country in which you are considering doing business.

Agency agreements

Clearly, the distinction between an agency and a distribution agreement can become blurred, especially if the agent is warehousing your goods. It is also extremely easy to fall out with an agent. Therefore, a carefully considered and properly drafted, written agency agreement is crucial for establishing the rights and obligations of both parties and for facilitating the resolution of disputes. The agreement needs to specify the following:

- the parties to the agreement;
- goods covered (especially whether the agent is to be allowed to repackage or otherwise alter items);
- product sales price;
- the period of the deal and the territory involved;
- how disputes between the exporter and the agent shall be resolved, which country's laws shall apply and whether and in what circumstances the dispute might go to arbitration;
- commission rates and payments for additional services;
- responsibility for:
  - collecting debts
  - transport of goods to customers
  - breakages and other spoilage

- local advertising and promotion
- after-sales service;
- whether a probationary period is to apply;
- whether secrecy is expected in relation to confidential information and the protection of intellectual property;
- requirements to disclose all relevant facts and to pass all sensitive documents back to your company on termination of the agreement;
- your right to inspect the agent's accounts and other records relating to your business;
- the precise extent of the agent's discretion to offer discounts, credit or special terms;
- responsibility for credit checks on potential customers;
- whether the agent is to participate in drafting promotional literature (if so, the agent will want payment for his or her contribution);
- how the agent's work will be evaluated (target-setting arrangements, for instance) and the consequences of poor performance;
- whether you will pay commission on orders received from the agent's territory that did not pass directly through the agent but which might be indirectly attributable to his or her work (repeat orders, for example). Regular customers will often seek to circumvent your local agent in order to obtain a lower price by dealing with you directly;
- arbitration provisions;
- termination arrangements;
- which country's law will apply to the contract;
- the agent's discretion to offer special terms to customers.

The agreement should spell out the meaning of key words and phrases (what is meant by 'exclusivity', for example), and detail when and in what circumstances the contract may be terminated.

Paragraphs specifying the rates of commission payable are particularly important. These should state the percentages available on various types of order, and the nature of the prices on which commissions will be calculated. Specify exactly when commission is payable: on receipt of an order, on delivery of the goods, or on final settlement of the resulting invoice. Is commission still payable if an order is cancelled at a late stage or if the customer's firm goes bankrupt? How frequently will accrued commission be handed over – monthly, quarterly, semi-annually or when?

Distribution (rather than agency) agreements might additionally include exclusivity clauses, details of allowable discounts, restrictions on the levels of final selling prices, responsibilities for technical product support and customer care, and provisions concerning liability for defective goods.

Agents versus distributors

An agent's operations are subject to your direct control, and may often be used for activities other than simply selling the goods (conducting or commissioning local market research or arranging after-sales service, for example – see below). Yet the use of distributors also has distinct advantages: fewer credit risks are involved (since the distributor acts as a principal); the distributor assumes full responsibility for storing and selling the item; little supervision is necessary, and it is possible to specify in the distribution agreement precise selling prices and the promotional methods to be used.

After-sales service and market research

After-sales service and customer care (see Chapter 7) can be arranged by your local representative (your agent, say) or undertaken by third parties whom you contract direct. The arguments for having your agent provide after-sales service are that:

- agents are near to end consumers and can communicate with them in languages they understand (fear of inadequate after-sales service from a British company could be a major incentive for foreign customers to choose domestically manufactured products);
- the agent has an incentive to ensure that goods are delivered in first class condition;
- the agent becomes 'locked into' dealing with your business.

However, the investment necessary to provide sound after-sales service can be extensive and agents who furnish these services must be trained, will require more extensive communications with your business than would otherwise be the case, and need guaranteed continuity of supply of spare parts. The agency contract stipulating who precisely shall be responsible (and financially liable) for the service will necessarily be complicated.

Using a local representative to conduct market research is cheap and convenient, but has disadvantages:

1. Agents and distributors will not normally have received any training in market research.

2. Your demands for information may cause them to respond flippantly, without conducting proper investigations, and hence to supply you with misleading information.
3. Agents and distributors obviously want your product to succeed in the local market, so their evaluations may lack objectivity.

Nevertheless, agents have direct and immediate access to final consumers and can observe at first hand their buying habits and demands. Also, they are ideally placed to analyse competitors' strengths and weaknesses. Another advantage is that customers will probably be more willing to respond to questions put to them by an agent (with whom they may regularly do business) than by outside research bodies. Indeed, customers may be pleased that your local representative is taking an interest in their special requirements.

Choosing an agent

Assistance available for locating potential agents is outlined in Chapter 3. The basic criteria to apply when choosing an agent are as follows:

- The agent's proven knowledge of local business conditions and practices.
- The agent's ability to conduct local marketing research.
- Whether the agent has contacts with local businesses capable of supplying specialist services to the exporting company (repair and after-sales service, for example).
- How easily the agent can be contacted.
- Whether the agent will represent competing firms and, if so, the incentives needed to encourage the agent to promote the exporter's products enthusiastically.
- How much information and feedback on matters such as consumer responses to the product, the quality of local delivery arrangements, whether local translations of operating instructions are satisfactory, etc, the agent can provide.
- How easily the calibre of the agent's work can be evaluated.
- The agent's track record, how long the firm has existed and its general business reputation.
- How extensively the agent covers the market; how many branch offices it has, their location and whether the agent can genuinely cover an entire country.
- Whether the agent possesses sufficient resources for the task: staff, showrooms, technical competence, storage facilities, etc.

- The ease with which the firm can control and motivate the agent. What control and motivational devices (for example, submission of market reports, inspection arrangements, commission and other incentive systems) can be built into the deal. Normally, the agent will be asked to prepare quarterly sales forecasts and to explain significant deviations of actual sales from these predictions. The agent should keep a record of enquiries received, calls made, customer complaints, etc and submit details on a monthly basis.

- Will the agent require a large amount of technical training about the product and sales training for promoting it effectively?

No serious agent will accept a client's assignments without first assessing the work of the client company and its long-term commitment to selling in the local market. Accordingly, you should supply detailed information not only about your products but also your recent performance in the UK, your business's strengths and the particular selling points of your output.

Because the agent is far away from your premises, he or she will inevitably need to make some decisions on your behalf without clearing them in advance. Accordingly, your agent has to be fully conversant with your company's policies regarding price, credit, delivery terms, cash and bulk purchasing discounts, availability of after-sales service, etc.

Motivating your agent

You need to keep in regular contact with your agent via meetings, telephone calls and regular submissions by the agent of reports detailing sales, prospects, market trends and so on. Also, you should regularly brief your agent about your current activities, changes in personnel, new product developments, marketing plans, etc. Some firms provide technical training to their foreign agents, jointly participate in trade fairs and exhibitions within the local market, and offer cash prizes and/or free holidays to agents achieving high levels of sales.

Chapter 6

Costing and Pricing

Choosing an appropriate price for your exported output is more difficult than for domestic sales for a number of reasons, notably the extent and possible unpredictability of the additional costs that exporting typically involves; lack of information on local market conditions; uncertain consumer responses to various levels of price; and foreign exchange rate fluctuations. Also, there are national differences in distributors' mark-ups, average credit periods, local inflation rates and governmental price controls.

Firms new to exporting frequently underestimate the extent of the additional expenditure that they will have to incur, resulting in significant underpricing of output with consequent financial losses on export sales. Apart from the obvious costs of special packaging, documentation, market research (including visits to the market), product modification and cargo and payments insurance, several other, less visible expenditures might be necessary, including:

- forward currency purchase costs (see below);
- special discounts that have to be offered in order to gain market entry;
- insurance claims costs;
- customs planning consultancy fees;
- pre-shipment inspection costs (see Chapter 7);
- costs of credit;
- miscellaneous bank charges;
- repackaging charges subsequent to customs examination;
- translation and interpreting costs;
- wharfage charges and clearing agents' expenses.

A further difficulty for companies selling to many foreign markets is deciding how to relate overheads to sales in particular countries. For example, what proportion of senior management time should be taken up by the firm's foreign operations? Should the business seek to cover all its costs including overheads ('full-cost' pricing) or merely the variable costs of foreign sales, regarding the latter as a bonus that contributes to total revenue but need not absorb overhead expenditures (these being fully recovered via the price charged on the domestic market).

Underpricing can lead to retaliation by irate local competitors (possibly even to accusations of 'dumping' and legal action in a local commercial court) and hence the unpleasant task of having to raise prices from their established low but inappropriate level. It is far easier to get consumers to accept price *reductions* than the other way round!

Selecting an export price

In deciding prices for selling in foreign markets you need to consider all the normal costs of production, promotion and transport, plus the special pricing requirements of the particular market concerned. The latter could include:

- brand images of the product (an item regarded as upmarket in one country may be considered downmarket in others);
- the strength of local competition and the ability and inclinations of competitors to change their prices quickly and by substantial amounts;
- whether the product is entirely new to a market (in which case a higher price might be charged);
- local conventions regarding discounts for bulk purchases and prompt payment;
- mark-ups and profit margins demanded by local retailers.

Define carefully your long-term objective in the market. Do you want a large market share (implying the need for a low price in conjunction with extensive advertising and sales promotions), or are you offering a high quality, top-end-of-the-market version of a locally available, low-priced product? In the latter case, the 'Britishness' of your output might allow the establishment of a prestige image for the product and enable you to charge a higher price.

To succeed in international markets you need to adopt the following procedure for determining the price at which you export your output.

1. Compile a list of the retail prices charged by competing firms in the local market. Two problems are involved here: first, the accurate identification of what *local consumers* perceive to be competing items (such perceptions may differ radically from

your own assumptions about what represents a comparable, competing product); and second, the assessment of price differences for the same brands in various types of outlet and in main cities and provincial towns. Regional price differences can be enormous. Many firms ask their banks to arrange for foreign branches to conduct price checks in local markets, or for an Embassy or Consulate to undertake this task. It is important to ensure that a proper range of regional price variations has been recorded. The same applies to type of outlet, since often the same item is sold in supermarkets, department stores, via mail-order catalogues or write-in newspaper advertisements, etc at significantly different prices.

2. Investigate local distribution systems to establish typical mark-ups of various channels and categories of retail outlet. Deducting the normal mark-up from the local price provides a target figure at which to supply the item to local intermediaries. It is also important to investigate the extent and nature of the discounts and credit terms offered by local competing firms.

3. List all the import duties and local sales taxes you will have to pay and the circumstances in which they can be (lawfully) avoided.

4. Sound out the opinions of local contacts 'in the field' (agents, retail store managers, etc) on the most appropriate price for the item.

Terms of sale

Customers need to know how much they will have to pay for your products and how, and the terms on which they will be delivered. The golden rule here is to adapt your pricing, delivery and payments arrangements to meet the customer's preferences. For foreign sales in the European Union this usually means quoting a local foreign currency price and delivering goods to the final customer on exactly the same terms and using the same delivery methods as a local firm. Why, otherwise, should the foreign customer bother with the inconvenience of importing goods from you rather than buying them from a nearby competitor?

INCOTERMS

Commercial documents such as invoices, letters of credit, contracts of sale, etc need to specify a price and terms of trade that define precisely the duties and obligations of buyer and seller and, in particular, the exact moment at which ownership of (and hence responsibility for) goods passes from one party to the other. The various options have numerous legal implications. National commercial laws may conflict and disagreeable arguments can arise concerning who is to pay for ancillary freight charges, consular fees, losses during transit, pilferage, and so on.

The International Chamber of Commerce (ICC) publishes a set of definitions of export delivery terms (INCOTERMS) for use in international trade. They are widely quoted and have a legal status in some countries. The definitions are updated periodically. Major INCOTERMS currently in use are as follows.

Ex Works (EXW). The goods are made available for the customer to collect from the exporter's (specified) premises in the firm's home country. Buyers take full responsibility for all transport and other risks and charges from the moment their consignments are collected.

Free on Board (FOB). The exporter (or freight forwarder, shipping company or other carrier) arranges for the consignment to be loaded on board a ship at a named port in the exporter's country. The buyer assumes responsibility for the goods the moment they pass over the ship's rail.

Free on Rail (FOR)/Free on Truck (FOT). These are the FOB equivalents for rail and road transport. FOB Airport can be used for air freight, following the same principles as ordinary FOB.

Free Carrier (FRC). This is the same as FOB but applies where the mode of transport cannot be clearly defined, for example when goods are loaded on to a trailer or into a container for collection by another firm. A particular location for collection will be specified.

Free Alongside Ship (FAS). The consignment is placed alongside a ship in a quay of a named port in the exporter's country and a port employee signs a declaration to this effect. From that moment onwards the customer is liable for losses resulting from theft, natural deterioration, fire or other damage. The customer has to pay for loading the goods on to the ship.

Ex Ship (EXS). Goods are made available to the customer on board a ship at a named foreign port of destination. Normally, the customer is responsible for unloading the goods. If not, the term used is *Ex Quay (EXQ)*.

Cost and Freight (C&F or CFR). The exporter pays all the transport charges (excluding insurance, which is the customer's obligation) required to deliver goods by sea to a named destination. The customer assumes the risk of loss or damage to the goods from the moment they pass over the ship's rail at the port of embarkation. For C&F equivalents using modes of transport other than ships, the term *OCP* might be used (or *DCP* if the goods travel in a container).

Delivered at Frontier (DAF). The customer takes responsibility for the consignment the moment it passes through a named frontier.

Cost, Insurance and Freight (CIF). This is the same as C&F but includes the requirement that the exporter and not the customer insures the goods to their final destination. For methods of transport other than sea, the term *CIP* might be used.

Carriage Paid To (CPT). Here, the exporter pays the freight charges to a named destination. However, the buyer assumes all risks of loss or damage to the goods from the moment the exporter has delivered them into the carrier's custody. If several carriers are involved, the risks of damage or loss pass to the buyer when the goods are delivered to the first carrier.

Carrier and Insurance Paid To (CIP). With CIP the seller has the same obligations as under CPT but, in addition, has to arrange and pay for cargo insurance.

Delivered Duty Paid (DDP). The exporter assumes *all* the risks and expenses involved in delivering the goods to the customer's premises. (DDP used to be known as Franco Domicile pricing.)

Without doubt, the best terms to quote are DDP in the buyer's national currency. Indeed, this is increasingly the norm in the European Single Market. Equally, *Ex Works* and other terms of delivery that impose extra work and inconvenience on customers are becoming unacceptable in very many countries. Customers think twice about importing an item that is available from domestic suppliers if the process of importing incurs significant financial and other costs.

Note that unless INCOTERMS have been incorporated into the domestic law of the relevant country (the laws of France and Germany, for example, assume that INCOTERM definitions represent normal trade custom), they do not automatically apply if there is no reference to them in the contract of sale or transport documents.

Thus, use of the term 'CIF Sydney' does not guarantee that the INCOTERMS definition will be employed to resolve any dispute regarding the meaning of 'CIF'; whereas appearance of the phrase 'CIF Sydney INCOTERMS' will ensure that the appropriate INCOTERM shall apply. Many disputes have arisen over whether the use of an INCOTERM was or was not intended by the contracting parties.

Currency fluctuations

Foreign exchange factors are critically important for pricing decisions since an appreciation in the currency of the exporting firm's country means that the importer will have to pay more local currency to purchase the foreign currency necessary to settle an invoice of a given size. If you quote selling prices in the currency of the importing country (to make it as convenient as possible for the residents to purchase the item) then you assume the risk of a fall in the importing country's exchange rate reducing your return when you come to convert accumulated foreign currency into domestic units.

In the latter situation you can sell to your bank, in advance, the foreign currency that your customers have been invoiced to pay. The bank will quote a fixed forward exchange rate for these transactions, which will apply to the conversions regardless of the actual spot exchange rate in force one or three months, say, from today.

The bank will demand a reward for its services and therefore will quote an exchange rate for forward currency transactions which differs from the current spot exchange rate by an amount sufficient to cover the bank's exposure to risk and enable it to make a profit. This obviously represents a significant additional cost.

An exporting firm that invoices in local currency and expects the spot exchange rate to move in its favour (so that it stands to raise more domestic currency when it eventually comes to convert than if it converted today) may decide not to bother with forward cover.

Another possibility available to an exporter scheduled to receive foreign currency payments over a long period is to enter an *option contract* with its bank whereby the exporter is given the right to sell to the bank foreign currency up to an agreed limit at a predetermined rate at any time within the next 12 months. If the spot exchange rate moves in one direction, the exporter will exercise the option; if it moves in the other, the option will not be taken up – forfeiting thereby the fee paid to the bank to purchase the option.

Other means for reducing currency risk are for firms to include renegotiation clauses in all sales contracts to enable them automatically to change the contract price in the event of significant exchange rate fluctuations; and the accumulation of interest-earning foreign currency balances in various countries, to be exchanged for other currencies at appropriate moments or used to purchase local products for subsequent exporting to other markets. Such devices impose additional costs and inconvenience on exporting companies relative to locally based rivals.

Costs of currency fluctuations

Apart from the need to take out expensive forward cover, currency fluctuations create other problems for exporters, as follows:

1. Regular price fluctuations (caused by changes in currency exchange rates) are entirely inappropriate for branded products for which the product price is a key factor in determining the brand's market image. Imported brands cannot compete effectively with locally produced outputs in these circumstances.
2. Test marketing in foreign markets becomes almost impossible since the price at which an item is test marketed might not be the price at which it will be sold following a large exchange rate fluctuation.
3. Currency uncertainty makes it difficult to introduce new products to a foreign market due to the need to change their prices in line with exchange rate movements.

Chapter 7

What to Export

Fitting the product to the foreign market

The 'product' that you sell is not just the physical item; it is also the way it is packaged, presented and branded. You may be fortunate enough to supply a product that will sell anywhere in exactly the same specification and format. Commonly, however, some degree of modification is required, though only of a minor nature in many cases. Hence, you need to find out about:

- particular technical standards that the item will have to satisfy in particular foreign markets;
- any climatic or other geographically related conditions that might affect the transportation, storage or usability of the product in the countries concerned;
- local preferences *vis-à-vis* product characteristics;
- relevant cultural or economic factors (for example, consumers in a poor Third World country might demand a basic 'no-frills' version of your product);
- local packaging regulations;
- after-sales service requirements, including warranty periods and the extents of warranty cover offered by rival firms.

Product modification

Ideally, you would be able to sell your basic product in an unmodified form in all your intended markets. Supplying a single, unmodified product leads to reduced stockholding costs (because demand in any particular market can be met from a single inventory of the same item), facilitates the development of technical expertise in a narrow field, and allows the interchangeability of spare parts and input components among products intended for different destinations.

Often, however, products cannot be sold abroad unless they are modified, perhaps because of variations in foreign tastes or local educational and literacy levels (for example, a 'simple to use' version of a high-tech product might be developed if local customers could have difficulty understanding the original model). Package sizes may need to differ for foreign markets; climatic conditions could be dramatically different from those found in the UK or disparate technical standards could apply. If your product has to be modified then hopefully only minor changes will be required (a new size or colour, length of warranty, carrying facilities, etc), though it has to be said that any alteration will involve additional costs.

Significant product modification, however, will present major organisational and managerial challenges to your firm. You have to develop experience and technical know-how of the modified item and how to promote it; duplication of effort could occur; additional advertising expenses will probably be necessary; and your overall product development activities may be held back as increasing amounts of time and other resources are devoted to issues pertaining to the special requirements of a particular national market.

The intensity of these problems might cause you to supply the same product to all markets unless there is a law or compulsory technical standard that prevents this. International sale of a standardised product may be feasible if:

- there exists a large market across several countries and where cultural differences do not necessitate adaptation;
- the product has a strong image, so consumers in new markets are likely to respond well to advertisements for the item;
- the fundamental need that the product aims to satisfy is basically the same in all foreign markets;
- after-sales service is easily standardised.

Technical standards
Sources of information on technical product standards are discussed in Chapter 3. The need to conform to different standards in different countries is a major irritant to exporters and can seriously disrupt international trade. Common technical standards exist within the USA and are being extended throughout NAFTA (North American Free Trade Agreement).

Standards are in the process of being harmonised across the European Union, although it will be some years before this enormous task is completed. An important test case (the *Cassis de Dijon* as it has become known) established the general principle that if a product is lawfully manufactured and approved for sale in one EU country then it *must* be accepted by the governmental standard authorities in other EU states, subject to its satisfying minimum, EU-harmonised product standards. However, this does not prevent customers insisting that goods be supplied to particular specifications, such as those laid down by a domestic trade association or industry standards body (the German DIN system, for instance).

Testing and certification

Your foreign customers might insist that your output conform to a certain quality standard (ISO 9000, for example) and/or to rigid design specifications, and reserve the right to reject consignments not meeting the stated requirements. An importer who receives goods that are not to the agreed specification can refuse to accept them and demand replacement. This is costly and troublesome to both parties to the contract so, to save the cost of shipping goods to their final destination only to have them turned away on design/quality grounds, it is not uncommon for export sales contracts to provide for the *pre-shipment inspection (PSI)* of the goods here in the UK at the premises of the exporting firm.

Both sides can benefit from PSI. The importer is able to monitor the quality of inputs as they leave the supplier's firm, and may be assured that appropriate legal and safety standards have been met. Sellers, conversely, demonstrate through their willingness to accept PSI their commitment to the market and to customer care.

Another reason for PSI is to enable the governments of importing countries to ensure that import consignments are genuine and not merely a device for transferring hard currency out of the country (for example, by importing crates marked 'machinery' but in fact only containing boxes of sand, and remitting hard currency payment to a foreign country to the value of the non-existent machinery). This form of PSI is most common in economically underdeveloped nations and is usually carried out by an organisation, *Société Générale de Surveillance SA*, specially constituted for this purpose. The document confirming that all is in order is known as a 'clean report of findings'.

Physical standards PSIs might be undertaken in accredited test centres in the exporter's country, or *in situ* at the exporter's premises by a representative of the importing firm.

Branding for export

The brand names under which your goods sell in foreign markets must be appropriate for the countries concerned (unmodified use of English brand names in nations with other languages not infrequently results in absurd, rude, culturally offensive or meaningless words) so it might be necessary to adopt a different brand name for the same product in each of your intended markets.

The essential advantage to having separate brand names for each country is that each name can be adapted to suit local circumstances (differing uses of the product, for example) so that local consumers may immediately relate to the particular image created by the brand. If you do opt for different brand identities in disparate markets, the names selected need to be distinct, easily recognisable, culture free, legally available and not subject to local restrictions.

A brand name is far more than a device to identify the supplier of a product; it is an advertisement in its own right and a means for arousing in consumers a set of emotions and mental images conducive to selling the item. Short, simple, easily read and easy to pronounce brand names are usually best for foreign markets. They should be memorable, and not readily confused with the brands of competing businesses.

Global brands

Where possible, most inexperienced exporters prefer to apply the same brand name everywhere as this can reduce worldwide advertising and other promotional expenditures, simplify marketing administration and facilitate the legal protection of the intellectual property embodied in the brand. It is still possible to use a common brand identity in different countries even if the product to which the brand name and image refers is itself differentiated in order to accommodate specific national requirements.

Protecting intellectual property

An unpleasant shock for some first-time exporters is to achieve outstanding success in a particular foreign country only to see their products blatantly copied and/or their brand names used by other firms! A brand is an example of a trade mark (a word, symbol or collection of words and/or symbols used to identify goods and to distinguish them from the outputs of other businesses) because brand identities emerge from words and symbols so that in a technical sense there is no essential difference between a 'trade mark' and a 'brand'. Thus, trade mark law and international conventions apply to this matter.

In some countries, the first user of a trade mark becomes its lawful owner. Elsewhere, formal registration with state authorities is required. Another important difference is between countries which require owners of registered trade marks to use them during specific time intervals (usually three to five years) or accept that other firms may appropriate them after the specified interval has elapsed.

Failure to take legal action to protect a brand name can result in it falling into the public domain as a generic product title. (Familiar examples of brands that have suffered this fate include kerosene, celluloid, thermos, aspirin and linoleum, all of which began as brands, but may now be used by any manufacturer.) This problem is especially severe when there is no generic term that adequately describes a broad type of product, resulting in the name of a well-known brand being commonly used as a proxy for the entire product category.

To avoid this happening it is necessary to use a proper noun for the brand name, immediately following the word describing the class of product (linoleum floor covering, for example). 'Brand piracy' is a significant issue in some countries, and includes the practices of:

- people other than the original brand name user registering the brand name of a firm just about to enter a country in which formal registration is necessary, and then 'selling' the brand name back to the business concerned;
- 'passing-off', namely making a slight change in the lettering of a brand name or a cosmetic alteration to the design of a logo in order to pretend that the item is the same as the original branded product.

Because not all countries recognise the principle that the person or organisation first using a brand name, logo, etc has legal ownership of the intellectual property embodied within it, it becomes necessary formally to register the firm's trade marks in *every* nation in which it intends doing business. This process can be extremely expensive and legal action to protect trade marks may also be very costly. In some countries it may be necessary to register a brand name at frequent intervals, with any brand name not re-registered in the correct manner becoming available to any other business.

For the European Union a Community Trade Mark (CTM) system is being introduced whereby it will soon be possible to obtain brand name protection in all EU nations via a single application. EU states have promised, moreover, to standardise their domestic intellectual property laws in order to avoid contradictions regarding what will and will not violate a registered trade mark.

The World Trade Organisation (WTO)
WTO is a Geneva-based international institution with 116 member countries, including all the industrialised nations. Its purpose is to cut

tariffs across the world, remove non-tariff trade barriers and generally encourage unfettered international trade. The last round of negotiations was conducted in Uruguay in 1989 (concluding in 1993) and, for the first time, incorporated agreements on measures for the international protection of intellectual property and the prohibition of trade in counterfeit goods. Under the Uruguay deal there is a minimum patent protection period of 20 years, regardless of where an item was invented or whether it is imported or locally produced, plus limitations on the use of compulsory licensing for patented products.

Compulsory licensing occurs when a patent holder does not produce and/or sell the item for a certain period (this varying according to the law of the country concerned – two years is typical) and another firm applies to a local court for permission to use the patent under licence from the inventor. The court can compel the latter to issue a licence on terms that the court considers reasonable. At present, there is a great deal of criticism that courts in some Third World and developing countries accept applications for compulsory licences far too easily. Further provisions of the Uruguay agreements concerning intellectual property are that all signatories must:

- offer copyright protection for at least 50 years from the creator's death (including protection for computer software and compiled databases);
- introduce laws to prevent the unauthorised disclosure of trade secrets;
- provide equal treatment for domestic and foreign intellectual property holders.

Developed countries were given one year in which to pass appropriate legislation, developing nations have five years, and the poorest countries ten years.

Warranties and customer care

Laws and customer expectations concerning warranty (guarantee) periods and the extents of warranty coverage vary from country to country, and it is essential to offer warranties comparable in length and scope to those available from competing firms.

In general, warranties represent an important export marketing tool. They attest the supplying firm's commitment to quality and customer service, promote the product and help to assuage consumers' doubts about a foreign business's commitment to provide maintenance facilities, spare parts, etc. The basic policy issue connected with the provision of guarantees to foreign customers is whether the after-sales service will be arranged by the supplying firm's local representative (an agent or distributor, for example) or by third parties which the firm contracts direct. This matter was discussed in Chapter 5.

Another important question is whether you should attempt to apply the same warranty conditions in all countries or vary the terms from nation to nation (over and above variations necessary in consequence of local law). Application of identical conditions is suitable for firms with a standardised product that is sold internationally in exactly the same form (especially if cross-border servicing might be required) and where buyer needs and use patterns are the same in all countries.

Note, however, that standardisation of warranty conditions does *not* offer economies of scale as typically occur with the standardisation of products or promotional messages. Also, there is no point in offering universal guarantees if the firm cannot arrange worldwide servicing. Arguments for varying warranty conditions are that:

- it enables the firm to respond to variations in the warranties offered by competing companies without imposing extra costs elsewhere;
- there are few cost advantages to standardisation;
- differing climatic and other use conditions can make it inappropriate to offer long guarantees in certain markets;
- it may be difficult for a firm supplying an item from several production units in various countries to maintain a uniform level of quality of output.

Customer care

Customer care is far more than after-sales service, although the latter is an essential part of the company's total customer service effort. Satisfied customers repeat their purchases and introduce new consumers to the firm. Moreover, it is much cheaper to obtain a repeat order than one for a completely new customer since no additional advertising or other selling effort is involved. A procedure for creating satisfaction among foreign customers is essential. Hence, a comprehensive audit of all your existing customer care activities is required to ensure that they are suitable for customers in foreign markets. The audit should examine:

- the availability of spare parts and servicing facilities;
- the length of product guarantees compared with those offered by competitors (see above);

- the clarity of translated instruction manuals;
- availability of post-purchase advice on the use of the product;
- efforts to maintain contact with existing foreign customers via mailshots, newsletters, etc in order to inform them of new models, product improvements, and so on;
- the accuracy and appearance of translated documents sent to the customer (invoices, for example);
- the ease with which foreign customers can place orders;
- the extent to which customers are consulted prior to modifying products;
- the extent to which information is given about ingredients, product uses, etc;
- the courtesy of company representatives;
- the availability of emergency help to customers;
- the convenience to customers of the systems through which they pay for their purchases.

Chapter 8

Promoting the Product

To the extent that you wish actively to seek out foreign customers rather than passively awaiting orders from abroad, you will need to promote your goods in foreign markets. Potential customers have to be made aware of your product, its qualities and characteristics, where and how it can be obtained, and what it will cost. You must create awareness of what your product offers, encourage buyers to try the goods, possibly maintain a favourable business image via public relations, and perhaps arrange point-of-sale inducements to purchase – just as for domestic sales. This could mean advertising the product and is extremely likely to involve attendance at foreign trade fairs and exhibitions. Sales promotions and international direct marketing may also be appropriate depending on the nature of the goods.

Advertising in foreign markets

Novice exporters will intuitively turn to advertising agencies for help with the production of advertisements suitable for foreign markets, the location and choice of the best media to carry messages, translation of promotional materials, and so on. However, there is no 'tablets of stone' requirement that this must always be the case, and doing it yourself might be feasible if your product is such that it is possible to use the same standardised advertisements in all the countries in which you intend doing business, rather than having to adapt them to meet the particular requirements of specific foreign markets.

Standardisation involves treating the world as one market, ignoring any apparent regional, cultural or national differences and promoting your output in exactly the same way in all states. Consumers with the same attitudes and buying habits are targeted in each nation.

Customisation of advertisements and of advertising campaigns, conversely, may be essential if there exist significant cultural differences affecting the consumption of the product in various countries, language translation difficulties or differences in the educational backgrounds of target groups of customers or national attitudes towards advertising. Alterations in advertising campaigns may take one or more of the following forms:

- *The use of different media.* For instance, listeners to commercial radio in one country may typically belong to a different socio-economic group than in others.
- *Changes in symbols*, such as using a male rather than a female model as the dominant figure in an advertisement. This may be necessary if males are the primary purchasers of the product in certain markets.
- *Changes in advertisement body copy.*
- *Changes in the fundamental selling proposition.* An example is the presentation of a bicycle as a leisure item in one market, a fashion accessory in another and a commuting vehicle elsewhere.

The main problem with customisation is the extra costs of having to tailor campaigns for various market segments, including translation costs, higher agency fees for foreign work and the cost of obtaining foreign currency to pay local media.

Advertising agencies

Each country has its own laws on advertising. In Europe, for instance, the use of superlatives is allowable in the UK, Belgium and Italy, but not in Germany or France (at least not on television). In the Netherlands, use of a superlative has to be backed up by factual evidence. Other practices that might or might not be illegal in particular areas of the world include:

- comparisons of an advertised item with competing products and/or mention of rival firms;
- advertising in foreign languages;
- use of pornography and sexual innuendo;
- advertising of 'health' foods, pharmaceuticals, war toys, alcohol and tobacco;
- use of children as models;
- the creative approaches that may be employed (for example, it is illegal in many countries to instil fear in consumers' minds in order to advertise products);
- the media permitted to carry advertisements and the amounts of advertising allowed in each.

International advertising agencies and domestic agencies in the country concerned will have detailed knowledge of these matters. They employ or have instant access to expert copywriters, translators, photographers, sales promotions specialists, film-makers, package designers, media planners, market researchers, etc, skilled and experienced in the international field. Only the largest businesses can afford to carry such people in-house. (Simply arranging and co-ordinating the services of these experts as external consultants and suppliers is itself a demanding task.)

Agencies may be 'full service', meaning that they cover the entire spectrum of advertising duties, or specialist (sometimes referred to as *à la carte*) dealing only with certain aspects of the advertising business, for example media relations, creativity and production, industrial goods advertising, television commercials, or whatever. Full service agencies have branch offices throughout the world. They provide clients with 'one-stop shopping' in that they will supply *all* the client's advertising needs (creative design of advertisements, production of literature, media relations, etc) from a single source and allow the client to avoid paying profit margins to the several different links in the advertising chain (copywriters, photographers, printers, and so on).

Despite the diverse and impressive activities of the large multinational agencies, the smaller local agency has survived – indeed prospered – in many countries. Small agencies, moreover, continue to attract significant volumes of work direct from clients in foreign states in addition to the assignments they undertake for local firms. Advantages to using a local agency include:

- its ability to give a foreign firm a local image;
- potential for close and effective liaison between the agency and local distribution agents and/or other representatives;
- possibly, a higher level of effort and commitment on the part of a local agency, which needs to offer better service in order to compete with larger and better known multinational rivals;
- flair and creativity that are sometimes absent in big international agencies.

The decision to use local agencies is easier perhaps for a client with a single product to be advertised in a limited number of countries. Conversely, advertisers with multiple brands to be promoted in many countries face several difficulties when using local agencies. The administrative burden of the agency selection process has to be undertaken many times, and it becomes necessary to communicate with control and appraise a large number of agencies.

Finding candidate agencies

The large multinational agencies are well known and have branches in most countries: a single domestic telephone call is all that is required to link you up with the agency's operations in any particular nation. Look in *Yellow Pages* for their telephone numbers. The *Advertisers Annual* lists hundreds of foreign advertising agencies, while a more extensive listing of advertising agencies throughout the world (plus their major clients) is contained in the annual *Macmillan Directory of International Advertisers and Agencies*.

A useful contact is the Institute of Practitioners in Advertising (IPA), which is a trade association representing advertising agencies, consultancies and other marketing services firms. The Institute is prepared to give enquirers a list of three or four agencies seemingly capable of satisfying their needs. However, the IPA exists primarily to represent its members and following the disclosure by the Institute of a few names and addresses of appropriate agencies, all further dealings are between you and the firms concerned.

Selecting an agency

Advertising agencies are not noted for their modesty and many will claim to possess expertise in all advertising specialities in all countries in all circumstances at all times! The reality is that each agency is likely to have greater experience and skill in certain fields and regions than elsewhere. It is essential, therefore, to examine carefully a candidate agency's past record, its list of clients and to take up references.

Key criteria to consider when choosing an agency are the candidates' experience of handling international programmes; their knowledge of and sensitivity towards cultural factors relevant in particular local markets; media evaluation and market research skills and facilities; and their creative approaches and standards for international campaigns. Specific questions to ask include the following:

- Does the agency possess an efficient translation service capable of identifying changes in the tone or meaning of an advertisement caused by translation?
- How intimate are the agency's contacts and relations with local media?
- How extensive are the agency's support services, such as advertisement pre-testing or access to mailing lists for direct marketing exercises?
- In the case of a multinational agency branch, how do local staff compare with the agency's staff in the client's home country?
- Is the agency capable of devising an entirely new advertising campaign for the firm's product without having to 'import' ideas

about the campaign from the advertisements the firm uses in its home country?

- What is the agency's track record *vis-à-vis* similar products in foreign markets?
- Does the agency offer adequate coverage of target market segments?

For large multinational agencies it is necessary to know: the income level and number of employees of each subsidiary in the countries where the client's products are to be advertised (this information is relevant considering the critical role of local subsidiaries in researching markets and implementing programmes); how subsidiaries communicate with head office; and what other types of account are handled from each subsidiary's location.

For small agencies, the client should request examples of the discounts it has been able to obtain when purchasing space in local media and when hiring outside specialist services. It is also reasonable to ask for details of the research techniques it uses to collect data (examples of questionnaires designed by the local agency, for instance).

How much to spend on foreign advertising

Special problems apply to the determination of advertising budgets for foreign sales. Observation of the advertising expenditures of foreign-based competitors is far harder than for domestic rivals and you may have little idea of the levels of outlay necessary to achieve your advertising goals (which themselves are likely to be less concrete for foreign than for domestic operations on account of your limited experience of local conditions and possibilities).

If you have a local representative (such as an agent) in the foreign country concerned, you may of course ask that person how much you need to spend on promotion. But a local representative (who will not be an expert on advertising) may have a totally unrealistic perception of the resources needed to achieve particular advertising targets in that market. Delays in reporting information could make it difficult to establish whether advertising money is being well spent.

A popular approach to setting foreign (and indeed domestic) advertising budgets is to allocate to the advertising function some fixed percentage of the value of quarterly sales. This guarantees that the firm only spends on advertising as much as it can afford, and the advertising effort becomes 'market led' in that resources are channelled primarily towards products that have genuine market appeal and which are therefore likely to do even better in future.

The percentage of sales approach prevents 'good money being thrown after bad', with each product being given the advertising it deserves. Expanding markets are automatically developed, and periods of exceptionally high sales create windfall income that can be used to experiment with new media, fresh creative strategies and high-risk, *avant-garde* approaches that otherwise could never be considered. A single, successful experiment might lead to a promotional breakthrough with enormous, long-term benefits for the advertising firm. The method is particularly suitable for low-cost, high-price (and hence relatively lower sales levels) items, since here there is a large margin available for advertising, which should of course boost sales.

The main disadvantage of the approach, of course, is that it ignores the possibility that extra spending on advertising may in fact be necessary when sales are declining, in order to reverse the trend. Other problems are that:

- the technique cannot be used to launch new products or to enter fresh markets;
- advertising costs differ significantly from country to country, so a greater level of expenditure may be needed to achieve a given level of performance in some markets than in others;
- the method's convenience and simplicity can encourage management not to bother investigating the relationships between advertising and sales or to analyse critically the overall effectiveness of its advertising campaigns.

Choice of method

There are, alas, no simple criteria to apply when selecting a budgeting technique. It may be possible, however, to group together those foreign markets which exhibit similar characteristics in relation to advertising (importance of certain media, size of market segments, rules and regulations, media costs, etc) and apply an intuitively appropriate method to each group. If advertising in one group performs better than elsewhere, the reason for this can then be analysed and applied to other markets.

In choosing a budgeting method it may be useful to consider the following factors:

- Expanding a large existing market share usually requires far higher advertising expenditures than increasing a small share of the market. Advertising to narrowly defined market segments generally needs fewer resources than tackling broadly based consumer groups. The percentage of sales technique might be best in either of these situations.

- The less satisfactory your current market situation in the foreign country the less useful is the simple percentage of sales approach.
- Soaring sales accompanied by constantly increasing advertising could provoke competitors into an 'advertising war' that you do not want and cannot afford. The percentage of sales approach should not be used if this might happen.

Translation of promotional materials

This is made easier if your advertisements, sales letters, maildrop leaflets and so on are drafted in simple language. It follows that colloquialisms, figures of speech, metaphors, technical terms and humorous expressions should always be avoided. The people who put together the initial copy should attempt to *think* in a multilingual way, assuming from the beginning that the material will be translated. The layouts into which copy is to be inserted should be large and open in order to accommodate the extra words sometimes created by translation (a translated text can be 25 to 30 per cent longer than the original).

To find a translator you can: (a) look in *Yellow Pages* (under the heading 'Translators and interpreters'); (b) contact the languages department of a local college (which may have teachers or advanced students willing to undertake ad hoc assignments for local firms); or (c) use the facilities of a professional institute. The main professional bodies in the field include the Institute of Linguists and the Institute of Translation and Interpreting (ITI).

Other sources of information concerning the availability of translation services include *The Register of Translators and Translating Agencies in the United Kingdom* (a directory of translators and agencies indexed by subject, language and geographical location), and the Association of Translation Companies, which acts as a clearing house for firms that require translation work.

Translators are usually best at translating *into* their native language from their adopted language rather than vice versa, so a native speaker is normally to be preferred. Translators need to be familiar with appropriate technical terms and to have access to directories and reference books covering their clients' industries.

The Institute of Linguists and the ITI

The Institute of Linguists is a professional body comprising more than 6,000 members qualified to use their language skills in industry, commerce and related fields. It maintains registers of translators and interpreters, and publishes a Directory listing those of its members available for freelance work.

The ITI has over 1,200 members capable of assisting businesses to satisfy their translating requirements. ITI publishes an annual index of translators classified by language and subject specialisation, and listing their addresses, telephone numbers and electronic communication and equipment details. Also, the Institute compiles lists of translators in various product/industry/country fields, which it will issue to prospective client companies.

ITI recommends that firms needing ad hoc translation services establish ongoing relationships with two or three other freelance translators, who will then become familiar with their work and (most importantly) the technical vocabulary they use. It is essential, the ITI argues, that: (a) clients establish personal contact with their translators; (b) the firm's requirements are specified clearly and precisely; (c) queries are discussed at the beginning of the exercise rather than at the end; and (d) adequate time is allowed for research, proofreading and the production of wordprocessed (or camera-ready) text.

Exhibiting

Trade fairs and exhibitions are one of the commonest and potentially most cost-effective means for promoting goods in foreign markets. Exhibiting can enable you to reach a concentrated group of possible customers in a few days rather than several months. The cost of exhibiting is also low compared with conventional advertising campaigns.

Exhibitions are especially useful for introducing new products to a market, since it is possible to obtain the initial reactions to new products of knowledgeable and attentive consumers, distributors, competitors, potential agents and other interested parties. Analysis of these first responses can be extremely valuable for deciding whether product modifications are necessary and/or how a full promotional campaign should proceed. Further advantages to exhibiting are that:

- orders might be obtained on the spot;
- small firms without extensive sales forces have the opportunity to present their outputs to large buying companies on the same face-to-face basis as large local rivals;
- the nature of the competition can be assessed;

- visitors' names and addresses may be used for subsequent mail-shots;
- potential agents will be among the visitors;
- although many technical specialists and company executives refuse to see or take telephone calls from outsiders who try to sell them things at their places of work, these same managers often *do* attend trade exhibitions. The customer goes to the exhibition in order to see the seller and not vice versa.

The problems involved

It is important not to become infatuated with exhibiting (especially considering the extent of the financial assistance available when attending exhibitions in other countries) and to recognise the problems involved. The cost, time and administrative effort needed to prepare an exhibition stand in a foreign country can be substantial, and you cannot guarantee that you will obtain the names and addresses of those callers to your stand who, subject to a follow-up letter or telephone call, will actually buy.

You may be unclear about how big a display to mount at any given exhibition, and having a large and attractive stand could simply induce competitors to do the same, thus wiping out the benefits of exhibiting. The employees who staff a stand at a foreign exhibition may be tempted to treat the event as a holiday – paying more attention to the social aspects of their involvement with the exhibition than to finding customers. Also, you want to know in advance as much as possible about the numbers and characteristics of the people who will visit the exhibition, their lengths of stay, needs, buying habits and so on.

At the time of writing, few *independently collated* research statistics are available concerning international exhibition audience sizes, visitors' behaviour or the impact of attending an exhibition on purchasing decisions. Exhibition organisers conduct such research for their own private use, but will not release information that could result in exhibitors drawing detrimental comparisons.

Selecting exhibitions

Clearly, not all exhibitions will be worth attending, and for certain types of product there are so many international exhibitions that it is physically impossible to attend them all. You should examine the following then decide which to support.

- How many orders are needed to cover the cost of exhibiting at the venue.

- Whether the venue is likely to attract a large attendance, the availability of nearby hotels, parking spaces, etc.
- Cost per square metre of stand space in comparison with other exhibitions, plus charges for ancillary services.
- The degree of overlap between target consumers and likely visitors to the exhibition.
- Whether the exhibition is well established (recently inaugurated exhibitions usually attract small attendances), and the track record of the exhibition organisers (their reputation, experience, etc).
- The extent of the availability of (a) useful information on the composition of past audiences and (b) lists of attenders and previous exhibitors.

Administrative matters

A number of practical issues need to be addressed when planning your participation in an exhibition, including:

- whether to undertake pre-exhibition promotions (for example, maildrops to people likely to visit the exhibition);
- visual presentation of the stand: colour scheme, headlines, etc;
- the best ratio of staff to stand space;
- style and quantity of leaflets, brochures and other promotional literature;
- how to evaluate the effectiveness of the firm's exhibition efforts (for example, how to measure the sales resulting from stand enquiries);
- budgetary control over exhibition activities: stand erection and removal, cleaning and insurance, printing of leaflets, hotel reservations for staff, hire of furniture, etc;
- booking of interpreters;
- deciding an exact position for the stand;
- selecting the right salespeople to staff the stand. Personnel must be fluent in the language of the country concerned, and technically knowledgeable about the product and the exhibiting firm. If senior managers from the exhibiting firm who are not fluent in the relevant language are to be present then an interpreter needs to be on hand to deal with problems. Interpreters engaged in person-to-person, 'on the spot' duties normally charge per day spent with the client. Note that face-to-face interpreting requires intense concentration (it is not possible to look up difficult technical words and phrases in a dictionary) and can involve substantial

amounts of stress – especially if heated discussions are involved. Thus, two interpreters may be needed for a full day's work, and both must be thoroughly briefed before the exhibition.

International direct marketing

Direct mail, telephone selling, catalogues and 'off-the-page' selling via cut-outs in newspaper and magazine advertisements are increasingly important as a selling medium throughout the world, especially in Western Europe and the USA. Indeed, the European Commission estimates that direct marketing today accounts for about a quarter of all commercial communication expenditure within the European Union. In the USA, direct marketing is the third largest advertising medium, after newspapers and TV.

Direct mail

Direct mail offers a flexible, selective and potentially highly cost-effective means for reaching foreign consumers. Messages can be addressed exclusively to a target market; advertising budgets may be concentrated on the most promising market segments; and it will be some time before competitors realise that you have launched a campaign. Also, the size, content, timing and geographical coverage of mailshots can be varied to suit national circumstances: the firm can spend as much or as little as necessary to achieve its aims. There are no media space or airtime restrictions and no copy or insertion deadlines to be met. All aspects of the direct mail process are subject to your immediate control, and you can experiment by varying the approach used in different countries.

It is hardly surprising, therefore, that direct mail activity is buoyant throughout the world. Freefone telephone facilities are available in most nations, and it is possible to quote an international 0800 freefone telephone number so that customers can ring free of charge in response to direct mail and other advertising campaigns.

Reasons for the expansion of the international direct mail industry include the increased number of independent households in many countries resulting from falling birth rates, higher divorce rates and increasing longevity; and fresh possibilities for the identification of distinct market segments among various types of family group. Direct mail, moreover, is the fastest growing medium for business-to-business advertising. According to Royal Mail International (RMI), two-thirds of Danish companies, three-quarters of German companies and half of all Spanish companies use direct mail for business-to-business campaigns.

Effective use of direct mail for business-to-business purposes requires the preparation of an accurate customer profile, including standard industry classification, size of target company (measured, for example, by turnover, number of employees or market share), the people to approach in each business (purchasing officer, project development engineer, product manager, etc), industry purchasing procedures and (where known) supplier selection criteria and the buying motives of prospective customers.

List broking

Commercial list brokers operate in all major trading nations. Information on list sourcing is available from the Direct Marketing Association and, in Europe, from the European Direct Marketing Association, which operates a chargeable international list search and co-ordination service. List broking is expanding particularly rapidly in France, the Netherlands and Italy. Europe's worse countries for list availability are Spain, Portugal and Greece.

List brokers take their profits by charging commissions to list owners (the standard international rate is 20 per cent), so that they can offer their services to clients either free of charge or at low cost (depending on the amount of work involved).

International mail despatch services

Royal Mail services include a *Printflow* facility for sending printed papers to foreign destinations. Printflow is available for maildrops, brochures, booklets, catalogues, directories, price lists, etc, though not for magnetic media such as computer disks or video tapes. The latter are handled through a similar scheme, the *Contract Airmail Packet Service*. Printflow has two forms:

1. *Printflow Air*, which guarantees the fastest possible transit times (three to five working days door to door) using scheduled air services.
2. *Printflow Surfacesaver*, which uses any convenient mode of transport to deliver mail. Transit time is five to seven days for near European destinations and seven to 14 days for longer journeys.

Mass mailings to Continental European destinations can occur via RMI's Airstream Europe service, which is for presorted printed paper – paid for on a kilogram weight basis. The Post Office will collect the mail from your premises. Postage rates are based on *total* weight and the number of letters. This saves having to weigh and stamp individual items. Airstream flies at least twice a day to key European destinations.

A business reply service is available for many foreign countries. All replies are sent to you by airmail. Cards and/or envelopes are acceptable. The weight of reply envelopes including contents must not exceed 20 grams. A standard design has to be used for cards and envelopes carried by the service. Royal Mail's 'International Admail' service is designed to improve clients' response rates on cross-border mailings by providing a local reply address for responses. Reply envelopes and cards are formatted in the style of the destination country so as to create a local image for the mailing company. The service costs a little more than the normal International Business Reply Service. Contact RMI for further information.

RMI's 'Direct Entry Service' enables your mail to be directly inserted into the postal service of the destination country. Envelopes look like local mail and provide a local return address for undelivered items. Importantly, the service allows you to operate a cash on delivery system when selling by mail order. This is especially important in Germany, where around 80 per cent of mail-order customers use cash on delivery.

Telemarketing

Telemarketing is today used both for consumer and business-to-business campaigns throughout the industrialised world. The telephone can be employed both to obtain orders and to conduct fast, low-cost market research. Telemarketing covers cold calling by salespeople, market surveys conducted by telephone, calls designed to compile databases of possible sales prospects, and follow-ups to customer requests for further information resulting from print and broadcast requirements. Currently, the majority of cross-border telemarketing campaigns focus on business-to-business contacts, essentially because of the combined telephone/fax/telex/database facilities that an increasing number of companies possess and, in consequence, the greater reliability of business-to-business communications.

To undertake international telemarketing you will need to engage a commercial telemarketing agency. Language skills are required, plus considerable experience in identifying decision makers in target companies. Telemarketing agencies can be engaged to receive the incoming calls resulting from a multi-country 0800 number maildrop campaign. Switchboard operators taking such calls have to be competent to respond in any of the languages involved and then pass the call to someone sufficiently *au fait* with the caller's language to be able to follow up the enquiry. The major telemarketing agencies now have transnational arrangements enabling the local country processing of incoming calls.

International sales promotions

Sales promotions such as money-off coupons, competitions, free draws, provision of an additional item for a small charge plus so many packet tops, etc can be an extremely effective tool for marketing in foreign countries. They may be used to stimulate impulse purchasing, encourage consumer loyalty, shift slow-moving stock, increase the frequency of repeat buying, smooth out seasonal demand, and generally draw attention to the firm and its products. Company expenditures on sales promotions have grown rapidly throughout the world. In Europe, for example, the European Commission estimates that the rate of growth of spending on sales promotions doubled that for conventional advertising throughout the period 1991–94.

There are, however, a number of serious practical difficulties confronting exporters who wish to employ sales promotions in foreign countries: in many nations the use of certain sales promotions techniques is regarded as unfair competition and as such subject to stringent legal control. Different (and sometimes conflicting) laws apply to these matters in various states. For instance, a money-off voucher is legal in Spain but not in Germany; a 'lower price for the next purchase' offer is legal in Belgium, illegal in Denmark and could be illegal in Italy; cross-product offers (buy one item and get a big price reduction on something else) are illegal in Luxembourg; and free draws cannot be used as easily in France as in most other states. In Germany and certain other countries free gifts and premiums are forbidden if they constitute a genuine incentive to buy.

Justifications for banning free gifts are that their distribution can be interpreted as a form of 'dumping', undertaken merely to force rival companies into liquidation, and that the true value of the promoted item is concealed.

The trade association for the sales promotion industry is the Institute of Sales Promotions, which will issue a list of its members interested in international consultancy work.

Chapter 9

Getting the Goods to the Customer

An immediate consequence of becoming involved with export is that you will have to arrange for the transportation of goods to foreign destinations in the most cost-effective way. The simplest way to ensure that your consignments are shipped safely to foreign customers, and that all relevant documentation is complete, is to use the services of a freight forwarder, although these have to be paid for and there is no reason in principle why you should not do the work yourself. Some firms begin their export activities using forwarders for all shipments, gradually assuming responsibility for the transportation of certain consignments as they gain experience of the tasks involved.

Before you do anything further, however, consider the possibility of sending goods abroad using the parcel post. Not everyone realises the extent of the Post Office's parcel services to destinations all over the world. Rates are reasonable; door-to-door pick up and delivery is normally possible; and a variety of specialised services are available.

There are, of course, size and weight restrictions (typically 20 kilos for West European destinations, 10 to 15 kilos elsewhere) and the customs authorities of the destination country must be willing to accept consignments sent in this way. An 'all-in' rate is charged which covers all transport and documentation. Insurance is available for an extra fee. If you are sending small consignments to numerous destinations, parcel post can be an attractive policy. Contact the Post Office for details.

Using a freight forwarder

Freight forwarders are businesses which specialise in the international movement of goods. Forwarders provide advice on:

- which modes of transport are most suitable for carrying a client firm's output taking account of its size, weight, characteristics and the urgency of the delivery;
- packaging and labelling;

• how and where to store consignments in foreign countries.

A forwarder will assume full responsibility for documentation and insurance, book air freight or ferry space for consignments, arrange for the collection of goods from sea ports, railway stations or container depots in other countries, and organise final road delivery. Major forwarders have their own transport fleets. Otherwise, they subcontract the actual carriage of goods to third parties in various countries.

Forwarders take their profits from fees charged to client companies, from commissions taken from the airlines, shipping companies, etc with which they book space, and from bulk discounts given by carriers and commercial warehouses in consequence of forwarders' groupage (consolidation) services, that is, their ability to combine numerous small shipments into a single large consignment going to a particular destination.

Substantial discounts are available for the bulk transportation of consolidation consignments, part of which the forwarder will pass back to small business clients in the form of lower freight prices. Moreover, a forwarder can often avoid the losses resulting from lorries having to return from particular destinations empty, since forwarders continuously liaise with each other and swap counter-directional loads.

The problem with groupage is that a specific consignment may be stored at the forwarder's collection depot for several days awaiting a consolidation into which it conveniently fits. Express service is always available, but only at a considerably higher fee.

Your only documentation requirement is to complete and hand to your forwarder a form called 'Export cargo shipping instructions' specifying details of the goods, their weight, dimensions, value and places of despatch and delivery. It might also require a statement of who is to be liable for various charges (such as insurance) once the consignment starts moving.

To find a freight forwarder contact the British International Freight Association (BIFA) or look in *Yellow Pages* under the heading, 'Freight forwarding and storage' which contains several subdivisions for forwarders specialising in particular fields. Some BIFA members participate in the Association's 'New Exporter Initiative' which offers novice exporters up to a maximum of one day's free consultancy on such matters as payment and sales terms, modes of transport, packaging and documentation.

Express services

Express services operate door to door and guarantee delivery within a specified time at a predetermined tariff. They specialise in smaller consignments (typically up to 32 kilos) and usually involve just a single carrying firm for the entire transport process. The term *integrator* is sometimes used to describe express operators who control or own all elements used in the transport chain (vehicles, aeroplanes, etc) door to door.

Integrators are able to employ hub-and-spoke systems whereby individual consignments are collected by van and delivered to a central 'hub' where they are sorted, bar-coded and their details scanned into the system, and then sent to a foreign hub by truck or aircraft. Local sorting for the foreign destination might be completed during the journey.

Packaging for export

Packaging is critically important for exporting because the degree of physical protection needed to safeguard items is often greater for exported goods than for domestic sales. Long sea or road journeys might be necessary, with much intermediate handling and sharp changes in climatic conditions. Also, foreign countries sometimes have laws requiring that packaging conform to certain standards and/or rules on the disposal or compulsory recycling of packaging materials. Germany, for example, has laws which require retailers, manufacturers and distributors to accept back all returned packaging, including crates, cardboard boxes, plastic containers and drums. Modifications to packages for various countries may be necessary in consequence of national differences in:

- the mechanical equipment used to handle goods in various countries;
- customer's goods inwards reception facilities (for example, whether they are prepared to break bulk at the doorstep);
- the quality of local warehousing facilities;
- consumer income levels. Low incomes imply lower usage rates of many products than in richer regions and hence smaller individual purchases;
- shopping habits. If consumers shop fortnightly rather than weekly, they will buy larger packages.

Normally, you will want to use the minimum packaging necessary to ensure that goods reach customers in a reasonable condition. Factors affecting your choice of package should include the cost of packaging materials, the amount of intermediate handling the goods will receive, the value of the item, whether an expensive package is necessary in order to enhance the image of the product, and breakage and spoilage costs (sometimes it pays to spend less on packaging and accept that more items will be lost or broken in transit).

The mode of transport is also relevant. Seafreight, for example, usually requires heavier packaging than freight shifted by other methods. Savings might be available through transporting in bulk and packing locally, particularly if a special pack is needed for the local market.

Insurance claims for damage to goods in transit will fail if it turns out that the goods were inadequately packaged. Losses can occur through pilferage, bad handling, shock (caused, for example, by a ship rolling in heavy seas or the shunting of railway wagons) or atmospheric changes. A problem relating to insurance claims for goods damaged in transit is that shock damage may not be immediately apparent. Outside containers may remain intact even though their contents have been broken, so it is difficult to establish precisely when the damage happened. Goods sent by air normally need less packing than goods shifted by surface transport.

It is not a good idea to state the contents of packages on outside covers as this encourages stealing. Rather, each package should simply bear a unique consignment number, the address of the consignee, plus an indicator of how many packages are contained in the shipment (for example, 2/4 indicates the second package of four).

For high value consignments it may be appropriate to use a false name for the recipient. Otherwise, a potential thief might know that the addressee regularly imports expensive items and be inclined to steal anything addressed to that customer.

There are internationally accepted symbols to indicate hazardous goods and/or special handling requirements. Further information on these can be obtained from the organisations mentioned in Advice on packaging on page 85. A *packing list* (also known as a 'weight list' or 'packing specification') is a statement of the goods supplied in a particular consignment, indicating which packages contain which goods and full details of the size, marketing and weight of each package.

National differences in packaging requirements

You need to establish at an early stage the packaging requirements for deliveries to specific countries as there are often special regulations concerning the materials used (prohibitions on flammable packaging or wood that does not carry a declaration that it is free of disease and insects, for example). Straw is forbidden as a means of packing imports in many countries (for long sea journeys straw can become damp and infested with disease and vermin), or is only accepted when accompanied by an approved disinfection certificate. Markings in addition to the normal shipping marks may also be needed.

Palletisation

A pallet is a flat tray upon which articles can be placed and secured, possibly by bolting or lashing. Carriers may request that even small items be palleted to allow mechanical handling (by fork-lift truck, for example). Freight forwarders and some road hauliers operate pallet pools to ensure the re-use of pallets after they reach their destinations. Otherwise, you may have to write off the cost of pallets as an inevitable expense of distribution.

Palleting greatly assists the speed, safety and general efficiency of loading and unloading procedures at docks and airports. Consequently, fewer dockside/airport warehousing facilities are necessary and aircraft/sea vessel turnaround is faster.

Types of package

Today the fibreboard carton is perhaps the most commonly used type of outer packaging. It is relatively cheap, light, yet able to withstand most transport handling. Suppliers of fibreboard cartons issue price lists defined in terms of bursting strength, weight limit and size, and whether the carton is single-, double- or triple-walled. Goods are packed into cartons which are then glued and reinforced with water-resistant tension strapping. Often, cartons are affixed to pallets, hence qualifying for the palletisation carriage price reductions offered by many ocean shipping companies.

Other than fibreboard, wooden cases and crates and metal drums are the most popular forms of packaging. If your foreign customer expresses a preference for packaging in wooden 'crates', make sure this means a skeleton wooden structure (the correct definition of the word) rather than fully enclosed wooden cases. Drums are frequently used to transport liquids, but note the lost space resulting from their circular section.

Containers

The standard container is 20 feet (6.10 metres) or 40 feet (12.20 metres) long, 8 feet (2.45 metres) wide and 8 feet 6 inches (2.60

metres) high. A 20-foot container can hold around 23 cubic metres of goods weighing up to about 20 tonnes. Note that 40-foot containers can hold double the volume, but *not* double the weight. Containers must be loaded evenly, with the centre of gravity in the middle of the unit (otherwise it is liable to tip when lifted). Heavy and well-packaged goods need to be placed underneath lighter ones. It is important to establish whether particular packages might give off moisture or odours, as these effects will be aggravated by the confinement of the goods in a sealed container. If you suspect that a particular package is likely to be inspected by the customs authorities then place it near to the door of the container.

The obvious problems with buying or leasing your own containers are: (a) their cost (both the initial outlay and subsequent expenditures on maintenance and insurance); and (b) what to do with an empty container after the load has reached its destination. Possibly, you could share the container with a local exporting company in the importing country, enabling that business to use the container for its shipments to Britain, or (at a cost) join one of the container pools operated by freight forwarders and other major carriers.

Advice on packaging

All the above sounds terribly offputting, but fortunately, organisations are available to help exporters arrange their packaging, notably the Research Association for the Paper and Board Printing and Packaging Industries (known as PIRA) and the British Standards Institution (BSI). PIRA will provide information on the properties of packaging materials and whether they conform to recognised standards. BSI is able to advise on climatic conditions likely to be encountered worldwide, with indications of the packing protection necessary.

Advice on export packaging is also available from freight forwarders and specialist export packing firms and from cargo insurance companies. Further information on packaging is available from the Institute of Packaging and the Institute of Physical Distribution Management (which publishes surveys of current packaging costs and practices). The main body concerned with palleting is the Timber Packaging and Pallet Confederation, which you can approach for advice.

Transport options

To the extent that you personally manage the transportation of consignments to foreign destinations you need to select the mode of transport to be used: road, rail, ro-ro ferry, air, regular shipping lines, or a mixture of these.

Road

In conjunction with ferry services and the Channel Tunnel this is the commonest method for transporting UK goods to 'near' destinations: the European Union, Scandinavia and parts of Central Europe. About 85 per cent of all road/ferry consignments are carried by third-party commercial road hauliers, the rest by vehicles owned by exporting firms.

Many UK road hauliers provide complete door-to-door collection and delivery services to and from Continental European destinations, including all the necessary documentation. A road haulier's receipt for accepting a consignment is called a *CMR note*. (CMR is the acronym for *Convention de Marchandises par Route*.) This records the contract of carriage, but does not provide evidence of ownership of the shipment. Additional documents are required for the road transportation of dangerous goods.

The CMR Convention lays down standard international contractual conditions for road transport, covering liability for loss or damage to goods and the maximum value of insurance claims against the haulier. You need, however, to check carefully who precisely will be responsible for extra costs incurred through ferry strikes, border delays, etc.

The TIR Convention

An international transport agreement known as the TIR (*Transports Internationaux Routiers*) Convention has for many years enabled road hauliers to seal their vehicles here in the UK, travel across national frontiers without interference, and have all customs clearance and documentation processed at the final delivery point. The TIR system became redundant within the European Single Market on 1 January 1993.

Under the Convention, responsibility for sealing TIR vehicles (or indeed any kind of container) loaded at the exporter's premises lies with the exporter rather than the hired carrier. The latter will provide a container seal which the exporter (not the driver) should ascertain is securely fixed. Each seal bears a unique number that needs to be recorded and subsequently quoted on transport documentation. The importer will check the seal on arrival and, if there is any sign of tampering, will write the details on the receipt given to the carrier and will retain the seal. Care in sealing is essential in order to try to pinpoint exactly where pilferage occurred. Seals themselves normally comprise steel bolts and/or heavy duty cables.

A vehicle becomes recognised for TIR purposes once it has been inspected by a national transport authority (the Department of Transport Vehicle Inspectorate in the UK) which then issues a certificate attesting that it is possible to seal the vehicle in such a manner as to guarantee the inviolability of its load. TIR certificated vehicles may be rigid, container-type lorries or (more commonly) canvas-covered semi-trailers where the canvas cover is fastened by a single hawser running through eyelets around the full perimeter of the cover and leading to a single seal.

The great advantage of door-to-door international road haulage is the avoidance of the need for transshipment of goods (having to unload and reload consignments between different modes of transport), thus reducing handling costs and pilferage losses. Final delivery by road is convenient for customers and flexible (routes and destinations can be altered quickly and at will). The problem is the possible absence of loads for return journeys. Road hauliers need to make the fullest use of vehicles (especially the cabs – 'tractors' – of articulated lorries) and will incorporate the costs of any time a vehicle is not earning money into quoted delivery charges.

Road and ferry

Complete vehicles or the trailers of articulated lorries may be transported on roll-on roll-off (ro-ro) vessels, which operate from numerous UK ports. Ro-ro services exist along the entire European coastline and in many coastal parts of the Middle and Far East.

Ro-ro is cheap because goods handling is reduced to the absolute minimum (no lifting gear is required and marshalling is easy) and because multi-million pound ferries can turn around extremely quickly. However, the effective payload of the trailer of an articulated lorry transported in this manner is substantially lower than, say, a rail or conventional sea container in consequence of the extra weight of the wheels and frame of the vehicle and the additional space these occupy. The large shipping companies provide integrated, door-to-door collection and delivery services throughout Europe and in a number of other parts of the world. Rates for ro-ro services depend on the length of the vehicle and whether it is accompanied, empty or loaded.

Rail

Completion of the Channel Tunnel has created continuity of transport between Britain and the Continent, providing direct access to rail systems extending to Central and Eastern Europe and beyond.

Goods may be sent using swapbody containers (that is, self-contained trailers that can be exchanged between vehicle cabs) or by direct 'piggyback' transport (the carriage of road vehicles by train). Piggybacking is already widely used by Italian, German and French exporters and, as the Tunnel system develops, it is sure to assume ever-increasing importance for businesses in the UK. Minimum rail freight journey times to European destinations using the Channel Tunnel are shown in Figure 9.1.

Transporting goods via the Channel Tunnel offers the exporter a number of significant advantages. Services are fast, convenient, reliable and unaffected by high seas, fog and other climatic conditions. Only one mode of transport is needed to reach selected markets and there is little intermediate handling during transit. Yet certain problems remain.

Several important regional markets are not easy to reach directly via the Tunnel system and, in consequence, BR freight charges will not be competitive in comparison with alternative modes of transport to such areas. These regional markets include most of the Netherlands and north-west Germany (served as they are by the highly efficient sea port at Rotterdam), Normandy, Brittany and other regions accessible from the ro-ro ferry services of the English south coast.

Moreover, rail transport is more economical the longer the distance involved. Thus, for journeys shorter than 250-300 miles, road/ferry freight services will probably continue to be substantially cheaper than rail, especially as they begin cutting their prices in response to the challenge to their business that the Channel Tunnel presents. This is particularly true where door-to-door delivery is required. Also, there are no distribution centres in the south of England between London and the UK portal. Hence, the transportation of goods to the Continent from locations near the south coast via the Tunnel requires sending them to London prior to their rail journey to France. South coast ports – Portsmouth, Southampton, Newhaven, Plymouth, and so on – have extensive ro-ro services, so obviously the Tunnel will not be attractive to businesses within striking distance of these towns.

Airfreight

In the past, airfreight has been used mostly for the transport of high value, low-bulk consignments. Increasingly, however, new and inexpensive aircraft are available capable of carrying larger and heavier

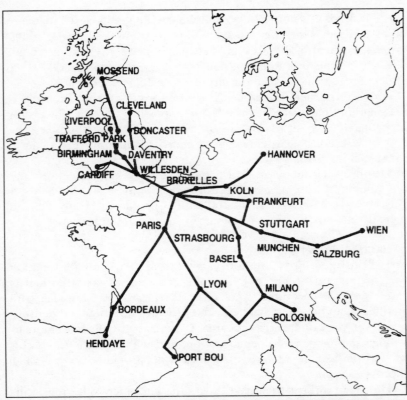

	London	Glasgow	Middlesbrough	Liverpool	Manchester	Birmingham	Cardiff
Novara	31	40	38	36	39	33	36
Milano	26	40	46	39	35	35	43
Strasbourg	16	28	34	25	23	21	31
Stuttgart	18	30	36	29	25	23	33
Basel	21	38	37	29	27	27	34
Bordeaux	21	38	35	28	27	27	32
Duisburg	17	41	36	29	30	30	33
Muizen (Belgium)	11	23	29	29	18	16	26
Paris	12	22	28	21	16	17	25
Mannheim	16	46	34	37	24	25	31
Lyon	23	34	40	33	28	30	37
Avignon	24	36	43	35	32	31	40
Perpignan	28	40	47	48	34	36	44

Source: Railfreight Distribution

Figure 9.1 Matrix of sample transit times in hours for freight traffic.

loads. Indeed, it is now cheaper to send certain goods by air than any other method. Moreover, speedy delivery means less stockholding, faster settlement of invoices and hence better use of working capital. Certain intermediate warehousing costs may also be avoided since goods can go straight from the airport to customers' premises.

Airfreight is therefore especially useful for goods where demand is seasonal or highly variable, as it becomes possible to meet new orders immediately without having to store goods in local warehouses. (The cost of warehousing may average as much as one-third the value of the stored items.)

Heathrow accounts for more cargo than any other UK airport, and the volume of airfreight passing through it is increasing by about 5 per cent each year. More than 100 airlines operate at Heathrow, and there are at least 400 freight forwarding agents in the area.

Arranging despatch

The British Airports Authority publishes a useful *Information Directory* that lists contact points and addresses of (a) cargo agents based around the three BAA airports (Heathrow, Gatwick and Stanstead), and (b) road hauliers who provide collection and delivery services in the London airports area. Cargo agents help consignors to arrange shipments and documentation, and will organise goods collection services if required. Airlines will provide lists of their approved agents.

The major airlines themselves also offer customer collection facilities, though you are perfectly at liberty to deliver cargo to airline terminals yourself. For certain airports you can deliver to airport container depots in city centres rather than to the actual airport.

Note that self-delivery (or hiring a local road haulier to shift the consignment) is not necessarily cheaper than using a freight forwarder or airline company because the latter might be able to collect loads from different customers in the same area on a certain day, and you do not have to pay for the return empty journey from the airport.

Booking space is very straightforward. You can offer your cargo directly to an airline (British Airways or Lufthansa, for example) or to a freight forwarder – who will almost certainly provide a consolidation (groupage) service. To book directly, you contact the airline and state when exactly the goods will arrive at the airport. The airline sends you a booking form (which might be called an 'instructions for despatch of goods' [IDG]) on which you specify who will be responsible for the payment of loading, freight and other fees and who will collect the goods on their arrival. Otherwise, a straightforward letter containing this information will normally be acceptable in lieu.

Airfreight rates

Most airlines belong to the International Air Transport Association (IATA) which sets common airfreight rates that in theory apply to all IATA members. In practice, however, price competition between airlines does exist (via special discounts and so on) and there is a considerable spread of airfreight prices. Airfreight rates are quoted by weight and volume, with the customer paying according to whichever is the higher value. In other words, for a given amount of money you get either so much space or a certain number of kilos. If, therefore, you are freighting a bulky yet light consignment you pay by volume and not by weight, and vice versa.

Discounts apply to cargo size, type of product, the route taken and the sizes and shapes of containers (which may be contoured to fit the fuselage of the aircraft).

The air waybill

This is a consignment note issued by the airline. It is not a document of title. However, provided the goods are addressed to the person (customer, agent, distributor) named on the air waybill and that person settles any outstanding freight or airport charges, the goods will be handed over on landing if the consignee has the order number and offers proof of identification. The air waybill is given to you by the airline company for completion by yourself (or your forwarder), and a copy of it accompanies the consignment. Three copies are required. One acts as an instruction to carry the goods; the second is a receipt for their safe transfer on to an aircraft; the third is for the consignee and must be signed by the latter as evidence of collection.

When the goods arrive the airline will notify the consignee (by telephone, fax or letter) or await collection depending on your initial instructions. Airports keep their own warehouses into which unclaimed goods are placed. A storage fee is then demanded if and when the goods are eventually collected.

Air charters

Price fixing does not apply to consignments big enough to justify chartering an entire aircraft, and there exists a market catering for the movement of exceptionally large or abnormal consignments that cannot be moved by normal scheduled air services. A 'single entity' air charter is the hire of the total carrying capacity of an aircraft. It is not always necessary, however, to hire a complete aeroplane. You may take a 'split charter' of part of the available space, alongside sections allotted to other clients. Charter brokers arrange air charters with aircraft owners on behalf of clients.

Charter rates vary widely depending on (a) the type of aircraft chartered, (b) the urgency of the trip, and (c) the time of year the aircraft is required. However, a chartered aircraft is not necessarily cheaper than scheduled freight services, since the charterer may have to pay for the entire round trip if the chartered plane needs to return empty.

Seafreight

You can send goods by sea using *liner services* (scheduled services which sail according to a strict timetable so that you know exactly when the ship will depart) and other vessels, sometimes referred to as *tramp ships*, that depart only when they have a full cargo. Liner services charge uniform rates applicable to all shipping companies. Tramp rates vary between vessels.

As for airfreight, seafreight charges are quoted on a unit weight/volume basis so you pay a certain rate for either so many kilograms weight or a corresponding number of cubic metres. Most rate cards equate one cubic metre to one metric tonne. You measure your load in these terms and pay according to which is the highest. Suppose, for example, the basic unit charge is £10 and your consignment is ten cubic metres and weighs three tonnes, you pay £100 for the shipment.

Supplementary charges may also be specified, possibly for additional fuel or extra unloading costs owing to port congestion, so be sure you know the total amount you may be called upon to pay. Storage charges incurred at docks (or airports) are referred to as 'demurrage'.

Arranging seafreight

To book space for a consignment you write to or telephone a shipping company (look in *Yellow Pages* under 'Shipping companies and agents') which then sends you a booking form and *standard shipping note* (SSN). The note advises the shipping company what is to happen to the goods on arrival at the foreign port, such as who will pick them up, who will pay unloading charges, whether the consignment is to be placed in a warehouse within the docks, etc.

An SSN also acts as a request to the destination port authorities to receive and handle the shipment. Accordingly, the port authorities must sign a copy of the SSN and return this to the exporter as proof of delivery. You can deliver a sealed, full container load (FCL) to the shipping company, or marked packages which the latter (for a charge) then inserts into containers owned by the ship. The latter is referred to as an LCL (less than full container load) service.

The contract between you and the shipping company is set out in a document known as a *bill of lading*. This also functions as (a) a receipt for the goods specifying whether they were loaded in a satisfactory or damaged condition, and (b) a document of title, meaning that the consignee named on the bill of lading has the legal right to claim the consignment. A clean bill of lading refers to goods received on board in apparently good condition and with no shortages. A short form bill of lading is one that does not show the shipping company's terms and conditions of carriage on the back. At least three copies are required: for you, for the shipping company and for transmission to the customer. The customer can transfer the right to collect the goods by endorsing the bill accordingly. Hence, a bill of lading is a 'quasi-negotiable' document of title.

If a bill of lading is lost, destroyed or not available for some other bona fide reason, or if perishable goods arrive before the buyer receives the bill of lading then the carrier may lawfully release the goods on receipt of a letter of indemnity from the party picking up the consignment. Suppose that the latter is not in fact the rightful owner of the goods and the true owner subsequently appears with a bill of lading. In this case the carrier has committed the unlawful act of 'conversion' and may be sued for damages by the rightful owner. The carrier in turn recovers the loss from the bank that issued the letter of indemnity.

As receipts, bills of lading provide only prima-facie evidence that a certain quantity was received on board, that packaging marks were in order, and that the goods were apparently in good condition. Nevertheless, it is up to the carrier to prove that the items stated were not in fact put on board or were not loaded in a certain condition. The ship's master need only attest to the receipt of goods in *seemingly* good condition and is not expected to investigate their inner qualities.

Special cargoes

Exceptionally large and indivisible loads require special planning. An air or seafreight charter may be appropriate and, importantly, the carrier must be given plenty of advance notice of the shipment because special lifting gear might be necessary for loading the consignment on to a ship, aircraft or railway carriage. Other special categories of cargo are high value goods and dangerous or obnoxious shipments. High value goods require special arrangements for stowage and supervision in transit, and probably a separate insurance contract.

Dangerous goods

All countries have laws relating to the carriage of dangerous goods, mostly based on United Nations recommendations. Also, the main international transport authorities such as the International Civil Aviation Organisation, the Central Office for International Rail Transport, and the International Maritime Organisation issue rules that incorporate UN suggestions. In Britain, PIRA (see page 85) is the government-recognised certifying body for dangerous goods packaging. Contact PIRA for more information.

Requirements for the packaging of dangerous goods are extremely stringent and the supplying firm must ensure they are satisfied prior to shipment. Otherwise the goods might be stopped in transit and the exporter may be liable to heavy penalties. Essentially, you must:

(a) state clearly that goods are dangerous, and classify them according to hazard using an internationally recognised coding system;
(b) use appropriate packaging, marking and labelling. Only packaging that has been performance tested in accordance with UN guidelines may be used;
(c) complete and sign a *dangerous goods note* to accompany the consignment which attests that the shipment has been properly classified, packed, marked and labelled. A freight forwarder will only agree to transport dangerous goods on condition that the exporter provides this declaration. Inclusion of the dangerous goods note in the shipping documents facilitates the advance booking of special handling equipment for dangerous consignments.

Dangerous goods by air

When transporting dangerous goods by air you are required by law to comply with regulations issued by the International Civil Aviation Organisation. These are highly technical and only to be interpreted by people who are expert in the field. They cover packaging standards and testing, marking and labelling, and require that the supplying firm (not the freight forwarder or cargo agent) declare that the goods are dangerous according to a precise format.

Common sense should indicate whether a particular type of good is 'dangerous'. However, apparently innocent products can contain dangerous substances. Examples are electrical apparatus incorporating alkaline batteries, barometers containing mercury, and anything with compressed gases, bleaches and/or magnetised materials. If you are in doubt, the Dangerous Goods Section of the Civil Aviation Authority will advise whether special packaging is needed and, indeed, whether air transport is possible.

Insuring the consignment

Cargo insurance (often referred to as marine insurance, regardless of the means of transport used) is available from your usual insurance broker. Normally it costs about 1 per cent of consignments, which are usually insured at CIF (cost, insurance and freight) value plus 10 per cent (to cover incidental expenses attached to the loss).

When purchasing cargo insurance be sure you understand (or have your broker carefully explain) what exactly you are getting. In particular, you need to know when precisely your responsibility for the safe transit of the goods ceases, what you are covered for and exclusions from the policy, and the periods within which claims must be registered. The latter are quite short, for example, 30 days for goods arriving by air.

Average

The word 'average' frequently crops up in the field of cargo insurance, and has a special meaning when used in this context. 'Average' means 'loss'. *Particular average* is a partial loss caused accidentally. *General average* is a partial loss deliberately incurred, for example, if an aircraft is in danger of crashing and the captain decides to jettison cargo in order to lighten the load. With general average, the loss is intended to benefit everyone; hence all parties are expected to contribute proportionately towards the cost, even if certain consignments have not been touched. Compensation for general average is available through standard cargo insurance policies (see below).

Most policies are 'With Particular Average' meaning that partial losses accidentally caused are fully covered. Otherwise, the policy is 'Free from Particular Average', so that claims for accidental, partial losses will not be met. Prior to 1974, each nation applied its own formula to the computation of general average. Since then, however, most policies have adhered to the 'York-Antwerp Rules', drafted by the International Law Association. Otherwise, general average is calculated according to the law of the country of the port of destination.

Types of cover

A policy can cover the transportation of a cargo from the warehouse of the seller to the warehouse of the foreign buyer, or just part of the journey. The standard form of policy used for Marine Insurance is the *Lloyds Marine Policy* (after Lloyds of London, the world's principal insurance organisation), which contains one of three sets of clauses, known as Institute Cargo Clauses A, B and C, that specify the cover the policy affords. Clause A provides the 'all risks' cover; B and C cover the particular risks, with C giving cover only against major catastrophes.

All three cover general average (see above) plus 'transit cover' against pre-shipment and post-shipment risks between a named inland source of supply and a named inland final destination. However, none of the three affords cover in respect of war damage or strikes; separate clauses must be inserted to insure against these risks.

It is not possible to insure unlawful cargos, or against damage resulting from the 'inherent vice' of the goods (such as innate propensity towards spontaneous combustion).

'Open cover' is available for exporters who continuously despatch goods to foreign destinations. Here, a single policy applies to all consignments, which are declared to the insurance company on a monthly or quarterly basis. Payment occurs as goods are shipped, not in advance. A 'floating policy' covers a number of prespecified shipments for which a lump-sum advance premium is payable. 'One-off' policies are known as *facultative* policies, and may be 'voyage' policies (whereby the cargo is insured from one specific place to another) or 'time' policies, in other words, the policy expires after a definite period. Note how the INCOTERMS (see Chapter 6) require that if goods are sold CIF then the *seller* must take out the insurance, which can have Institute Cargo Clause A, B or C. For a C&F (cost and freight) contract neither party need take out insurance, and the goods travel at the buyer's risk.

Policies frequently specify 'franchises and excesses'. A *franchise* in this context is any percentage loss beneath which the underwriter will not pay compensation; for example, if the loss is less than, say, 5 per cent of the value of the goods, the exporting firm must bear this itself. An *excess* is an amount deducted from the compensation payable, for example, if the exporter is liable for the first £250 of the total loss.

Shortlanding certificates

If a carrier (shipping company, road haulier, etc) discharges a consignment of lower quantity than stated on the transportation document (a bill of lading, for example), the carrier or its agent should issue a certificate confirming the short landing. This certificate is necessary in order to lodge an insurance claim in respect of the missing cargo.

Carriers are (not surprisingly) reluctant to issue shortlanded certificates as, by doing so, they imply acceptance of liability for the loss. Hence, they will insist on first conducting their own investigations (for example, to establish whether the missing units were accidentally discharged at a previous destination). Some carriers will offer ex-gratia payments of, say, 50 per cent of the shortfall in order to avoid having to deal with a claim from the customer's insurer. Import duty is, of course, not payable on the proportion of the cargo shortlanded.

Chapter 10

Doing the Paperwork

Virtually all the documentation associated with exporting can be subcontracted to outsiders such as freight forwarders, shipping agents, international road hauliers, customs agents and other specialist firms. However, you need to commission the services of these businesses, and it is useful to know the basics of the necessary paperwork if only to be able to monitor outsiders' work and make sure they are doing a good job.

Documentation is important. A research study commissioned by the European Commission estimated that documentation typically accounts for between 4 and 7 per cent of a business's export costs – rising to as much as 15 per cent if the documents contain errors. This is not really surprising when you consider the many public and private bodies requiring information about shipments of goods between countries. Interested parties include:

- final recipients of consignments;
- employees of warehouses where goods are to be stored;
- foreign agents and distributors;
- managers of container depots or marshalling yards;
- dock, railway terminal or airport authorities;
- carriers of goods (road hauliers, airline companies, ferry services, etc);
- banks instructed to release money needed to pay for goods only after evidence that their shipment has been transmitted;
- handlers of the goods who need to identify particular consignments;
- VAT authorities;
- government departments that collect data on imports and exports.

It follows that a large number of documents is needed to export goods, and the more intermediaries (hauliers, ferry companies, distributors, etc) handling the goods the greater the importance of accurate documentation.

Differences in goods descriptions, discrepancies in order and consignment numbers, uncompleted boxes on customs forms, absence of instructions for disposal of shipments on completion of their journeys and so on, may cause long delays and serious financial losses. Goods arriving at sea ports or rail or air terminals without proper identification will be placed in local warehouses which charge storage fees to the parties eventually collecting them. Late delivery to consumers creates bad customer relations and eventual loss of orders.

Obtaining the order

Initial export documents are no different from those needed for a domestic sale. On receipt of an enquiry you will need to check the feasibility of its fulfilment and, if you decide to quote, to issue a pro-forma invoice (a draft invoice containing full details of price and delivery terms offered, even though the customer has yet to place an order). The potential importing firm might need a pro-forma invoice in order to approach (a) its national import licensing and foreign exchange control authorities for permission to go ahead with the transaction, and (b) its bank to ask for a letter of credit.

Next, you should consider whether you require a licence to export the goods.

Export licences

UK residents are allowed to export nearly all items – without any need to obtain special government permission – via the 'open general licence' system, that is, it is assumed that it is perfectly in order for you to export the goods, so you simply go ahead. Certain goods, however, may only be exported following the issue of a specific licence by the DTI's Export Licensing Unit. Examples of goods subject to licensing control are antiques and works of art, firearms and military equipment, aircraft, atomic energy materials, high-technology goods such as computers, metalworking machinery, scientific instruments, 'strategic' metals and minerals, and a number of chemicals and categories of petroleum equipment.

The onus is on you to find out whether you need a licence, so it is important to check if you are in any doubt. Indeed, fines, delays and perhaps even the seizure of the goods may be involved if you attempt to export goods subject to licensing controls. Licences may be required for the export of some categories of item to any destination or just to particular destinations.

Declaration of exports

All exports except for parcel post and certain samples must be declared to the exporter's national customs authority on the appropriate document, quoting the relevant HS number (Harmonised Description and Coding System). For parcel post the declaration is embodied in the document completed by the exporter when contracting its national postal service to deliver the parcel. Note how a 'parcel' might actually be a large and quite heavy consignment (up to 4 metres long and 100 kg in weight in some circumstances).

Sales to EU customers are declared on your quarterly VAT returns (an outline of the procedure is given on pages 107–8) and, if your annual sales to other EU countries exceed a certain threshold (currently £150,000), you are required to complete customs form C1501 'Supplementary Declaration for Despatches' (SDD) on a monthly basis. These are known as INTRASTAT declarations and must be taken seriously: HM Customs imposes fines on companies that fail to complete SDDs. The forms are available from local VAT offices and have to be sent to the customs authorities within ten working days of the month end.

For non-EU exports you report their value through either:

- SAD forms (see page 102);
- the 'low-value procedure' whereby for shipments with monetary values below a certain threshold (revised periodically) you can evidence the exports using a carrier's receipt (a standard shipping note (SSN), for example), provided the goods are not subject to UK excise duty;
- the 'simplified clearance procedure' under which you pre-register with HM Customs, which allocates a unique Customs Registration Number (CRN) to your firm. Then you declare each export shipment within 14 days of it having occurred. Every shipment must be accompanied by a document stating the CRN plus a consignment number to identify the load.

Large and regular exporters are allowed to make special arrangements with HM Customs for declaring shipments on a periodic basis.

The contract of sale

This is perhaps the most important document of all and needs to incorporate details of the price of the goods, parties to the sale, delivery terms – CIF (cost, insurance and freight), DDP (delivered duty paid), etc – the latest despatch date, the mode of transport to be used and the method of payment. It should also specify which country's laws are to apply to the contract, details of letter of credit arrangements (where applicable), and all the documents required by the buyer prior to payment. Further clauses that might be included are:

- a *price escalation clause* entitling the supplier to increase the selling price by any unforeseen additional production or transport costs incurred between the dates of quotation and delivery;
- a *penalty clause* for late delivery;
- an *arbitration clause* specifying that a certain international body shall resolve any disagreement arising from the contract;
- a *force majeure clause* defining each party's rights and duties following the occurrence of events beyond their control, for example, that the contract ceases to be binding if there are dock strikes, political disturbances in either country, sudden imposition of foreign exchange controls, etc;
- a *reservation (retention) of title clause* (see Chapter 12). These are sometimes referred to as Romalpa clauses, after the name of a famous test case which established their legitimacy.

The commercial invoice

This should include all the commercial information used for a domestic transaction, plus the following:

1. Full details of the method of carriage and where and when the goods will arrive.
2. Details of the markings and contents of packages.
3. Weight and measurements of each delivery.
4. Precise terms of sale.
5. Where appropriate, the import licence number and a declaration of the country of origin.

The consular invoice

A number of countries (especially the poorer, underdeveloped countries) require foreign firms that sell to their residents to furnish a 'consular invoice'. This is an attestation by a representative of the government of the importer's country who is based in the exporter's country that the goods specified in the pro-forma reasonably correspond to the price stated. The purpose of the consular invoice is to prevent deliberate underpricing and hence the avoidance of import duties, or overpricing in order to transfer large amounts of foreign exchange out of the country.

Typically, the attesting person is an employee of the Embassy or Consulate of the country concerned. He or she will make an assessment based on published market data, local trade practice, trade magazines, price lists of other firms, invoices for similar items issued by alternative suppliers, and possibly an expert, independent opinion in appropriate cases (for example, for high value consignments where fraud is suspected). Fees are payable for each attestation.

Certain nations require foreign suppliers to produce 'certificates of origin' which state the place of origin of the goods (including where they were processed and where raw materials and/or input components came from) and that the goods have not passed through specified nations. Chambers of Commerce can verify certificates of origin, although foreign Embassies or Consulates might have to be involved.

The Single Administrative Document (SAD)

The SAD is the basic customs document that has to be completed for all goods exported to non-EU countries. It contains 47 boxes, although not every one of these has to be completed. Filling in an SAD can be complicated, but advice on how to do this is contained in the publication *The UK Tariff,* published by HMSO, and available in main public libraries. Eight copies are required, the first two going to HM Customs at the point of departure. You retain the third copy; the remainder are sent to the customs authorities of the importing country and to the customer. Box 33 of the SAD requires you to specify the appropriate HS number (see page 43).

Movement certificates

Exports from the EU to non-EU countries with which the EU has special trade agreements require a 'movement certificate' to enable them to benefit from preferential rates of tariff available to imports from the EU. Examples are *form EUR 1* needed when exporting to Switzerland, Cyprus, Malta and certain East European nations, and the *ATR form* used when exporting to Turkey. You obtain movement certificates from HM Customs and Excise, which produces a pamphlet explaining the scheme and how to complete the document.

Clean report of findings

This is a document issued by pre-shipment inspection agencies (see Chapter 7) confirming that the correct quantities have been shipped and that the price is reasonable for the level of quality of the goods. Sometimes a clean report of findings is necessary before the government of the importing country will release to the importer the foreign exchange needed to pay for the consignment.

ATA carnets

A carnet is a document which enables you to move goods temporarily between different countries without having to pay any tax or customs duties. Carnets are used extensively for shifting exhibition materials, samples to be shown to customers, demonstration equipment and other working materials. Chambers of Commerce that belong to the International Chamber of Commerce are allowed to issue to businesses 'ATA' (*admission temporaire*) carnets valid for most countries. The exporter has to deposit with the Chamber of Commerce the value of the highest customs duty that would otherwise be payable on the goods, this being returned when the items come back to the home country. If the terms of the carnet are violated, the Chamber of Commerce pays the deposit over to the customs authorities of the relevant country.

UK exporters can take advantage of the (chargeable) *ATA Carnet Indemnity scheme* established by the London Chamber of Commerce and a number of Lloyds underwriters. Under this scheme the exporter does not have to turn over any cash in order to provide the security deposit; instead, a charge is registered against the assets of the exporting firm. If anything goes wrong, the Chamber must settle up with the appropriate customs authorities *before* attempting to recover outstanding amounts from the exporter. Note the usefulness of carnets for the movement of substantial consignments sent on what, in effect, is a sale-or-return basis following inspection by the potential customer.

Other important documents

Further documents which are explained in other chapters are the cargo insurance certificate, transport documents such as bills of lading or air waybills, and the dangerous goods note where appropriate. Other documents that might be necessary are:

- *performance bonds* (bid bonds) whereby a firm tendering for a foreign contract has to deposit with the potential client a certain sum of money that is forfeit if the bid is successful but the bidding firm then decides it does not want (or is not capable of performing) the work. The purpose of a bid bond is to ensure that a bid is serious and not submitted frivolously;
- *health/sanitary certificates* required by the customs authorities of many countries for imports of foodstuffs, livestock and horticultural products. These can be obtained from the Ministry of Agriculture, Fisheries and Food;
- *conformity certificates* (also known as certificates of manufacture and free sale) which confirm that goods conform to relevant technical standards in the buyer's country. It might be necessary to have a certificate countersigned by a Chamber of Commerce or UK Consulate of the foreign country.

SITPRO

There is a government department – the Board for the Simplification of International Trade Procedures (SITPRO) – specifically established to simplify international trading documents and procedures and to provide useful, free advice on export documentation to UK businesses.

SITPRO also produces and sells standard forms guaranteed acceptable to the authorities of foreign states, plus the software needed for computerised systems. If you belong to a Chamber of Commerce, you may be able to purchase these standard SITPRO documents (such as shipping and dangerous goods notes, airfreight letters of instruction, bank letter of credit forms, and so on) at a reduced price.

SITPRO publishes a series of do-it-yourself manuals for export documentation, each containing sample forms, checklists, information on shipping marks, etc. It also produces a booklet explaining how to cut the costs of export administration.

The SITPRO overlay system

The purpose of SITPRO standard forms is to enable the exporter to complete just one or two core documents which can then be photocopied and used for multiple documentation purposes. You type all the necessary information on the basic form (the SITPRO master) and then apply the various plastic overlays supplied in the SITPRO package to photocopy relevant information on to particular documents. The invoice overlay, for example, will block out all material not required for a commercial invoice, while positioning the information that is actually needed into appropriate places, leaving you with a headed and neatly constructed invoice.

All SITPRO documents are designed to satisfy international specifications (the International Chamber of Commerce, European customs agreements, the United Nations plus the various regional trading blocs) and can be generated using an ordinary photocopier.

Despite the enormous improvements in the speed and efficiency of document processing that the SITPRO overlay system provides, photocopying remains a tedious duty and, in view of the fact that most small businesses today have a desktop computer, the use of commercial software packages for the production of export forms is increasingly common. SITPRO has a computerised system and privately constructed systems are also available. Suppliers advertise in export magazines and in the publications of trade associations and Chambers of Commerce. The experience acquired through using a computerised system for export documentation often leads firms to progress to EDI (see below) for the transmission of information rather than relying on hard copy.

Electronic Data Interchange (EDI)

Computerised facsimile document transmission systems are increasingly used for the interchange of export/import documentation. For the individual exporter, a computerised documentation system ensures that invoices and air waybill numbers coincide, that identical goods descriptions apply to all documents, that booking sheets relate to the proper loads, etc. All the information for documenting a consignment to a known customer or of a particular product type is quickly assembled; payments cycles are shortened and errors (and hence clerical costs) reduced.

The fully integrated electronic mail exchange of documents between exporters, customers, public authorities, banks, carriers, agents and distributors, customs, dock and harbour authorities, etc is called Electronic Data Interchange (EDI). A major advantage of EDI is that it avoids the need to rekey information into different computers at various stages in the chain of distribution. Hence, there is no chance of errors (which cause transport delays and hold-ups in payment) creeping into documents through frequent rekeying. The main problem, of course, is the incompatibility of computer hardware and systems making it difficult for computers in different countries to interconnect.

Customs clearance

Customer satisfaction will be greatly enhanced if you do everything in your power to facilitate the importation of your product into the country concerned. Indeed, if you quote a DDP price you automatically assume responsibility for customs clearance. Accordingly you should:

- make sure you have identified exactly the right HS number. Import licences may be available to your customer for some HS categories but not for others. The level of duty payable might vary enormously among neighbouring HS classifications; foreign exchange restrictions could apply to certain HS codes. Also, additional sales taxes might be imposed on specific HS groupings within the importer's country;
- establish whether an import licence is necessary;
- ascertain whether any special inspections will be required as the goods enter the importer's country. A number of developing countries operate 'Comprehensive Import Supervision Schemes' whereby government agencies inspect particular classes of imports *vis-à-vis* their quantity, quality and the reasonableness of the stated price, and will allow customs clearance only if satisfied that everything is in order;
- identify the formula according to which import duty will be calculated;
- ensure that goods are properly marked and labelled in accordance with local legislation.

Declaring imports in the customer's country

It is the importer's responsibility to tell the customs authorities of the country of importation that the goods are being imported and to present the correct information. Goods will be held up in customs until the duty on them has been paid (either by the importer or the exporter as determined by the contract of sale), unless they are going to a bonded warehouse or freezone (see pages 108–9).

'Entry forms' must be completed informing customs of the quantity, type, value and destination of the consignment. Customs officers have the right to inspect goods and accompanying documents and, if they inspect, the cost of resulting damage to packing cases, etc has to be borne by the importer. Entry forms may be lodged a few days prior to importation in order to speed up processing. Otherwise, they must normally be deposited within 14 days of arrival or they will be sent to a special warehouse and storage charges will be imposed.

Customs entry may involve the production of a carnet (see page 103).

Transaction values

GATT rules require that 'transaction value' be used as the basis for the assessment of customs duties. This means the price paid by the importer plus the following if not included in the price:

- Packaging costs and commissions incurred by the importer.
- Royalties or licence fees payable as a condition of the sale.
- The value of any help provided free of charge by the importer to the exporter in the production or marketing of the goods.

Countervailing duties

If the customs authorities of the importing country believe that you are 'dumping' goods in that nation, that is selling at a price below the price charged in the UK (plus transport and foreign distribution costs), they are allowed, under GATT regulations, to impose special import taxes (known as countervailing duties) on your product.

The European Union has its own rules on this matter. When deciding whether the export price charged represents dumping, the 'price' considered is that which the exporting firm charges to non-related local distributors, not the price paid by the final customers. A non-related customer is one who is not tied to the supplying firm via an agency agreement or exclusive dealership. If all distributors are in fact 'related' to the supplying foreign firm, the price charged to end consumers is used.

VAT and European Union customers

Currently, exports to the European Community are free of UK Value Added Tax, but are subject to import tax (now known as 'acquisition tax') levied at the domestic rate of VAT applicable in the importing EU country. This tax is levied on the CIF value of the imported goods. However, firms selling across national EU borders must (a) quote the customer's VAT number on each invoice, (b) prepare a quarterly return stating the total sales to each VAT-registered customer, and (c) be able to provide a full description of the goods.

If you do not know your customer's VAT number, you can obtain it via your local UK VAT office. Only sales invoices quoting these numbers are zero-rated for UK VAT purposes. If foreign EU customers are not registered for VAT in their own countries, you have to charge them the standard UK rate (unless the goods themselves are exempt or zero-rated), and declare this to the UK authorities.

For mail-order distance selling you must charge UK VAT to any non-VAT-registered foreign EU customer *until* your annual sales in each country exceed certain threshold levels, at which point you must register with their VAT authorities and thereafter charge local VAT and hand this over to the VAT authorities in each country in which the threshold is exceeded. Unfortunately, threshold values vary from country to country.

European Community VAT rules are in a state of flux and it is essential that you contact your local VAT office to establish your precise obligations. Note, moreover, that the VAT return (together with INTRASTAT forms in appropriate circumstances – see page 100) is today the principal means whereby you inform the UK statistical authorities of the value of your foreign EU imports and exports (replacing the Single Administrative Document which was phased out for EU sales following the completion of the Single Market).

There are no customs duties on goods moving between EU member states, although excise duties are payable on certain items (alcohol, for instance). Customs posts will continue to exist at the national frontiers of some (but not all) EU nations for the collection of statistical information on intra-Community trade and for health and police controls.

Release of dutiable imports

Dutiable imports can be brought into a country and stored in a *bonded warehouse* free of import duty and only have to pay duty when they are released. While in a bonded warehouse the goods can be repackaged, manipulated and further processed. If the goods are re-exported then no duty at all is payable. Bonded warehouses are supervised by the customs authorities of the country in question.

A *freeport* serves the same function as a bonded warehouse but comprises a designated wider area at a seaport where goods can be stored and worked on free of duty. Inland *freezones* are the same but usually located near airports. Other names for freezones are 'export processing zones' and 'investment promotion zones'. Today, there are several hundred freeports/zones throughout the world, accounting for anything up to 10 per cent of international trade. Freezones vary in relation to the extent of tax relief afforded to the firms operating within them. In several Pacific Rim countries freezones offer total exemption from *all* forms of taxation (not just customs duties), and have minimal health and safety regulations. Significant investment incentives (cash grants, generous depreciation allowances, etc) might be available.

Freezone warehousing is especially valuable where the imported goods are subject to a quota restriction since you can be sure that consignments will not be refused entry to the country on arrival, if a quota threshold happens to have been exceeded. The items can be stored duty free until the next quota period.

Customs planning

National customs administrations operate disparate practices in relation to a number of matters, including:

- their interpretation of the HS number to which items should be ascribed;
- whether duty payable on goods released from bonded warehouses is charged at the currency exchange rate prevailing at the moment of release or the moment of entry to the warehouse;
- whether (as in the United States) the authorities reserve the right to charge *ad valorum* tariffs on the basis of local market selling prices rather than on the importer's buying price.

It is essential that the importing firm minimise the amount of duty it is obliged to pay on imported items, so careful 'customs planning' is necessary to optimise the importer's position. This can be achieved by delaying payment of duties until the last permissible moment; by applying that description of the imported goods which classifies them in the lowest possible tariff category; and possibly by importing products as subassemblies rather than as finished items.

Customs planning is particularly important (and complicated) for firms whose products include imported raw materials and/or components since the range of potential reliefs, scope for redefining the characters of goods, possibilities for altering the route by which items enter a country (which can greatly affect their liability for duty), methods of valuing imported goods for tax purposes, and so on, increase greatly.

Customs planning services are offered by the large accountancy firms and by specialist *customs brokers* who act on behalf of third parties (importers or exporters) in order to clear imported consignments for domestic use or to place them in bonded warehouses. Customs brokers are more common in some countries than in others, and occupy an especially important role in Southern Europe (for imports from outside the EU). In certain nations they have to be registered with the state customs authorities. Customs brokers complete all the paperwork associated with customs entry, provide financial guarantees to national tax authorities *vis-à-vis* the full eventual payment of duties on imported goods, and advise clients on aspects of customs planning.

Re-exporting imported goods

If you import items from outside the EU and subsequently re-export the same items to a non-EU country, you can claim back some or all of the import duty you paid on them. The repayment is called *drawback*, which is only available if, at the time of importation, there was a clear intention to re-export the goods (normally within six months, although this can be extended in reasonable circumstances).

Similarly, you are entitled to *inward processing relief* from import duty if you import non-EU goods, work on them and then sell them outside the EU. This need not require a specific Customs authorisation prior to import provided you have a sound tracking system that follows goods from import, through manufacturing, packaging and export, that has been approved by the Customs authorities. Inward processing relief is a complex matter and advice should be sought from HM Customs as soon as you decide on entering into this type of transaction.

An alternative to claiming drawback is to use the *anticipated equivalence scheme* whereby you are allowed to import another item of the same value without paying duty on it.

Outward processing relief (OPR)

This applies to firms that send goods to non-EU countries for processing or repair and subsequent return to the United Kingdom or another EU nation. To apply, you write to your local Customs Office using a prescribed form of words (available from local Customs) and, if OPR is authorised, you have only to pay import duty on the repair or processing costs incurred abroad, not the total value of the re-imports (referred to as *compensating products*). A successful application receives an authorisation number valid for one year.

Summary: the export process from start to finish

Here is a summary of the main steps in the export process. The precise order of events will vary from situation to situation and firm to firm.

1. Receive an enquiry from abroad. Check your product's specification against the importing country's technical product standards.
2. Prepare a quotation. Determine the delivery terms (FOB, CIF, etc) and issue a pro-forma invoice.
3. Receive the order. Establish whether an export and/or an import licence is required and take appropriate action.
4. Accept the order, specifying a delivery date. Draft a contract of sale and have the customer acknowledge acceptance of its conditions.
5. Arrange for pre-shipment inspection and/or the issue of a certificate of origin and consular invoice as appropriate.
6. If quoting a foreign currency price, take out forward exchange cover.
7. Arrange transport. Book cargo space. Complete a carrier's instructions form (an SSN for example). Obtain the carrier's receipt for the shipment (bill of lading, air waybill, CMR note, etc).
8. Arrange cargo insurance and select Institute Cargo Clause A, B or C. Take out payments insurance or arrange for invoices to be purchased by a credit factor.
9. Inform UK Customs of the transaction via:
   (a) your VAT return and INTRASTAT form for EU sales;
   (b) a customs form for non-EU exports, using either the pre-entry procedure for declarations prior to shipment or the Simplified Clearance Procedure for declarations after shipment (provided a pre-shipment advice has been deposited).
10. If applicable, prepare a dangerous goods note and advise carriers of the nature of hazardous items. Complete other special documents.
11. Prepare a packing list.
12. Issue a commercial invoice.
13. Arrange customs entry in the importer's country. Pay customs duties (if this is your responsibility), complete an entry form and, if applicable, place the goods in a bonded warehouse.
14. Collect payment (via open account, bill of exchange, letter of credit, etc).

Chapter 11

Financing the Transaction

If you have total confidence in a customer's ability and willingness to pay then it is appropriate for you to accept payment by cheque, in an agreed currency, on the customer's receipt of the goods. This is known as *open account trading*. The cheque itself may be drawn on the buyer or its bank (as a banker's draft). To speed payment (bearing in mind that international cheque clearance can take a long time) you can ask your foreign customer to arrange for its own bank to authorise a UK bank to pay you immediately following the customer's receipt of the consignment. Authorisation may occur via telephone, fax, telex or airmail letter.

Unfortunately, foreign sales typically involve factors that make open account trading virtually impossible. Buyers may be unknown, credit checks might be unreliable, and there are risks of foreign governments suddenly imposing restrictions on the availability of foreign currency to importers. Insurance against non-payment by open account customers is available in certain, restricted circumstances, but quite expensive. Credit factoring (see Chapter 12) of open account invoices may be possible, although a high discount will be charged and the factoring company will want to be completely sure that the foreign customer will definitely settle the invoice.

Using bills of exchange

In view of these problems, it is hardly surprising that the great majority of non-EU export sales are paid for using methods other than simple open account cheque clearance. For low value transactions you could insist on payment in advance, or that the customer send you a post-dated banker's draft (dated for payment immediately following delivery) prior to your despatching the goods. High value sales require more extensive documentation, although you should not be put off by this because your bank will handle all the technical details.

These alternative methods typically involve the preparation by the seller of a bill of exchange. This is a document drafted by the seller of goods, instructing the buyer to pay the seller an amount of money either on receipt of the bill or (more commonly) on a specified date in the future (for example, in three months' time). A bill that requires payment immediately or within three days of acceptance (see below) is called a *sight bill* or *draft*; one that is to be settled in the future is referred to as a *term*, *usance* or *tenor bill*. You need not worry about having to originate these complicated sounding documents because all the banks have their own standard format for bills of exchange and offer extensive help and advice on how to use them. The commonest application of bills is for documentary collections.

Documentary collections

Here you complete a bill of exchange and give it to your own bank, together with various documents (such as the insurance certificate, invoice, transit and any other documents) required by the customer prior to taking delivery. Your bank now sends the bill to the importer's bank, which presents it and the relevant documents to the customer. If the bill is a sight bill, the customer settles it at once. If it is a term bill, the customer accepts it by signing the bill (to acknowledge existence of the debt) and it is then returned to your bank, which now becomes responsible for collecting the money. All the documents which provide title to the goods are handled by your bank, which will only release them to the customer at the time of payment.

Technically, all bills of exchange remain drafts until they are formally accepted, though nowadays the word 'bill' is generally used for all circumstances.

Raising money against an accepted bill of exchange

Other possibilities for an accepted term bill of exchange are as follows:

(a) Sell it to your bank at a discount (bills of exchange are negotiable instruments) hence raising immediate cash to finance the production and delivery of the goods. Your bank then collects the money when the bill matures. Thus, the bank assumes the risk of non-payment. This is sometimes called an *acceptance credit* transaction.

(b) Keep the bill until it falls due for payment and collect the money yourself.

(c) Borrow money from your bank using the accepted bill as security.

In the last case your bank might want a guarantee that the bill will definitely be settled, for example, by requiring the importer's bank to promise to honour the bill if the importer defaults. The term *avalised bill of exchange* is applied to a bill that carries such an undertaking. If the bill is not avalised and the buyer defaults, your bank will still expect your company to repay the loan. This is an example of 'finance with recourse', a situation in which money obtained from a bank to finance an export transaction can be claimed back by the bank if the customer eventually defaults. 'Finance without recourse' occurs when the bank assumes the entire risk of customer non-payment.

The International Chamber of Commerce publishes a set of guidelines – *Uniform Rules for Collection* – for the use of bills of exchange, which can be legally binding if a contract so stipulates.

Default on a bill of exchange

If a foreign customer defaults on a bill of exchange and it is your responsibility to collect the money, the first step towards recovery through local courts is to have the bill protested. This means getting a notary public (a local person legally qualified to attest and certify documents) to ask the customer for payment or reasons for non-payment. The reasons are put into a formal deed of protest which your solicitor then places before a local court as evidence of dishonour.

Documentary letters of credit

A letter of credit is an undertaking issued by the customer's bank to pay a stated sum of money to the exporter, provided certain pre-specified conditions are met. These conditions normally relate to the receipt by the importer's bank of a number of properly completed documents (including documents of title) relating to the transaction. The most important documents are as follows:

- Transport documents, such as bills of lading, air waybills, road or rail consignment notes, parcel post receipts, etc, which give evidence that the goods are in transit.
- A commercial invoice (see Chapter 10) giving a full description of the goods and terms of payment.
- An insurance certificate. For letter of credit and documentary collection purposes you need a full insurance certificate; a broker's cover note will not normally do. However, if you use open cover (defined in the section on credit insurance later in the

chapter) you can draw up a certificate yourself on a standard form printed and already endorsed by the insurance company.
- Where appropriate, dangerous goods notices, packing lists, pre-inspection certificates, bank indemnities, etc.
- Bills of exchange.

The procedure for letter of credit settlement is as follows:

1. Your customer approaches his or her bank and asks it to open a letter of credit in your favour. This letter of credit will specify when payment is to be made (such as on presentation of documents or at a later date) and which documents must be submitted prior to the paying bank releasing the money. On issuing the letter of credit the bank assumes liability for the debt.

2. You – or more commonly the local UK bank (known as the advising bank) that is handling the transaction – are informed that the credit has been opened and of the exact conditions to be met prior to releasing the money. You must read these conditions carefully, noting the expiry date and any special terms relating to:
   (a) place of payment (if the money is to be paid into a non-UK bank there could be a few days' delay before it is transmitted to Britain);
   (b) liability for costs incurred over and above the value of the credit, for example, for freight hold-ups or inspection fees;
   (c) how claused transport documents (for example, if a carrier writes on a consignment note that goods were received in a damaged condition) will affect the validity of the letter of credit;
   (d) the means of transport to be used;
   (e) the latest date for despatch of the consignment.

3. The goods are sent off and the documents forwarded to the bank that is to pay you the money. A bill of exchange may or may not be included in the documents depending on the precise terms of the credit.

4. On receipt of the documents the paying bank checks them and, if they are in order, releases payment. Alternatively, if payment is to be through a bill of exchange, the bank accepts and returns this on behalf of the customer. In the latter case it is the bank and not the customer that honours the bill of exchange when it matures.

5. The customer's bank passes the documents to the customer, provided the customer has paid in to the bank the amount due or has negotiated an overdraft.

The importer's bank may ask you for an indemnity against the buyer deciding not to pay for the goods, for example, if they are short measure or of unacceptably low quality. If you give an indemnity, you will be paid promptly, but must then reimburse the importer's bank – with interest – if anything goes wrong. Do *not* issue indemnities under normal circumstances and never without carefully discussing the matter with your own bank.

A confirmed letter of credit is one whose settlement has been guaranteed by a UK bank. You are paid directly by the UK confirming bank, which then collects the money from the foreign bank issuing the credit. The confirming bank has no claim on you if the credit is not honoured. Currently, nearly all letters of credit are irrevocable, meaning that they cannot be arbitrarily cancelled by the customer.

The International Chamber of Commerce has published a set of model rules for the use of letters of credit. These are binding on all parties if the credit bears an endorsement stating that it is 'Subject to ICC Uniform Customs and Practice for Documentary Credits'.

Customers in the European Union

Do not expect EU customers to respond kindly to demands for letters of credit. Why should they? Such complications are not necessary when buying from local suppliers, and customers' own banks will probably require that appropriate funds are placed on deposit before issuing letters of credit. Hence, working capital is forgone, and the foreign firm's borrowing ability may consequently be affected! Letters of credit must themselves be paid for, and the administrative work involved (especially for arranging confirmation by a UK bank) can be expensive. There are arrangement fees, bank and interest charges, all of which are conventionally borne by the buyer.

Errors in letters of credit

Banks have a vested interest in not parting with money until the last possible moment, so they will not remit payment unless the documents are *exactly* correct. (The legal principle that allows them to behave in this way is known as the 'doctrine of strict compliance'.) Thus, goods descriptions on invoices and advice notes must tie up; dates must coincide; payment terms (DDP, CIF, etc) have to be clearly stated; words and figures must tally, and so on. The following errors are especially common:

- unsigned documents (though under international agreements photocopies of signed documents are perfectly acceptable);

FINANCING THE TRANSACTION

- misspelt company names and addresses;
- inadequate descriptions of the goods included in particular consignments;
- wrong addresses for goods destinations;
- contradictions in documents, such as mentioning a bill of lading (see Chapter 9) in one document and an air waybill in another.

A number of surveys have indicated that about half of all letters of credit are not settled by paying banks on first presentation because of errors in documentation.

Special forms of documentary credit

Back-to-back (counter) credits involve two separate letters of credit. The first is in favour of the exporting company, which now instructs its own bank to issue a second letter of credit in favour of one of the exporter's own suppliers (for example, to provide raw materials necessary to produce the goods).

A *deferred payment* credit is a letter of credit specially designed to give importers extra time to pay. The deferment period may terminate on a predetermined date regardless of when the goods are despatched, or be due for settlement a certain number of days after delivery.

A *red clause* credit authorises the importer's bank to pay the exporter before presentation of the documents. Other names for red clause credits are 'packing credits' and 'anticipatory credits'.

Revolving credits are letters of credit used to cover a number of consignments when the exporter wishes to avoid opening a series of individual credits. Revolving credits apply to a number of different consignments within an agreed limit. Hence, the credit amount is automatically renewed without formal amendment.

A *standby credit* is a letter of credit with an extended period for payment. Under the arrangement, the importer's bank stands ready to honour the credit if the exporter can prove that the importing firm has failed to meet its obligations. The purpose of a standby letter of credit is to allow the participating businesses to trade on an open account basis, so that the credit is never actually used except in the event of default by the buyer.

Standby credits are non-performance documents used only when the importer does not perform a contracted duty. Conversely, the standard documentary letters of credit previously referred to are performance documents, that is, payment occurs given the presentation to a bank of satisfactory documents proving export of the goods. In other words, a standby credit comes into play if something does not happen rather than when something does.

Transferable credits are letters used by intermediaries in the export trade which enable the intermediary to transfer part of the money released under the credit direct to the intermediary's supplier(s).

Performance guarantees

The converse to a letter of credit from the buyer's point of view is the need to be assured that the supplier has the technical and financial resources to deliver the goods on time. Thus, the exporter may be required to provide a bid bond (see Chapter 10) issued by the exporter's bank at the time the exporter tenders for a large contract. The bid bond (typically representing 2 to 3 per cent of contract value) is forfeit if the contract is awarded to the bidding firm which then decides not to accept it.

Forfaiting

This is a means of financing the export of expensive capital goods which customers are not obliged to finish paying for until a long time in the future – as in the international construction industry, for example. Suppliers must invest large sums *now* although buyers will pay by instalments as the project proceeds, with the final instalment falling due anything up to two years *after* the project's completion.

To raise money to pay for the substantial initial investment that the exporter will have to make to resource the project, the exporting firm may draft not one but a series of bills of exchange – each with a different time to maturity – for acceptance by the purchaser. The first bill – representing the customer's first instalment – may be payable three months after beginning the project; the second bill (for the second instalment) may be due six months after that; the third a few months later, and so on. Following their acceptance, these bills may then be discounted *en bloc* by the exporter, today, at the exporter's bank in exchange for a cash payment.

In the past, forfaiting has been used exclusively for high value projects. Today, it is used extensively for smaller amounts, although a minimum fee over and above the cost of funds for the deal will be required to ensure that administrative expenses are fully covered.

Forfaiting is especially popular for financing export deals of between two and five years' duration. It is 'finance without recourse' in that the bank purchasing the bills assumes full responsibility for collecting the money, and has no comeback against the exporter.

However, the exporter's bank will probably insist that the bills of exchange be avalised (see page 114). Finance is available for any period between six months and ten years, depending on the foreign country concerned and the bank's assessment of the risks associated with the project. Specific advantages to forfaiting are as follows:

- Exporters avoid the (typically) 10 to 15 per cent non-indemnifiable risk normally required on credit insurance policies (see the section on credit insurance on page 120) plus the lengthy delays typical of insurance settlements.
- The amount available to the exporter is known with certainty and there are no risks of currency exchange rate depreciation (critically important if you invoice in local currency). As bills of exchange are sold to the bank at today's known rate of discount, the exporter pays what is in effect a fixed rate of interest on the money raised.
- Forward planning and budgeting are made easier since all costs and revenues are predetermined.
- The cost of this finance can be quite low compared with other sources (conventional bank loans for instance).
- Although the exporter is effectively borrowing money to finance the project, the sale of a bill of exchange is not regarded in law as borrowing *per se*, and so does not appear as such on the exporter's balance sheet.

Nearly all the major banks offer forfaiting services, and you can shop around for the best terms. The field is increasingly competitive, with many foreign banks now bidding for UK exporters' forfaiting business. To select a bank for forfaiting purposes, compare (a) the discount rates at which various banks will purchase the bills (banks will quote different rates according to their assessments of the risk attached to your business), and (b) banks' surcharges for delays in payment caused by administrative problems such as errors in documents, postal delays, etc (some banks add up to five days' extra interest for these).

You should also examine the question of commitment fees. These arise if you are uncertain about how and when the customer will eventually want to pay, so you can ask a forfaiter to agree to purchase relevant bills of exchange as they arise, without determining a precise date for settlement. In this case a commitment fee will be payable from the date of your request until the moment you present the bills for purchase by the forfaiter.

Credit insurance

The governments of most OECD countries operate export credit guarantee systems that offer residents low-cost insurance against customer default. This has led to allegations that certain countries are subsidising the exports of resident companies unfairly and that there exists an 'uneven playing field' where export credit insurance is concerned. Accordingly, the OECD countries have now agreed to limit the amounts of support they offer, and within the European Union a proposed Directive has been drafted with the intention of harmonising the ways in which member states use credit guarantees as a means of promoting exports.

In the United Kingdom it used to be the case that the government-owned Export Credits Guarantee Department (ECGD) provided the full range of payments insurance services. However, in 1991 a Dutch private sector company, NCM Ltd, took over all ECGD's short-term business (credit periods of up to two years), leaving the state-controlled ECGD to direct its activities mainly towards the insurance of payments for exports of capital goods to non-OECD nations.

Initially, the government wanted all NCM's operations to be entirely self-financing but, realising that it would not be possible for NCM to re-insure itself against potential losses in high-risk markets which, nevertheless, provided many opportunities for UK exporters (Nigeria, for example), the government agreed to 'top up' NCM's provision of short-term cover for these difficult countries until 1997. Thereafter, the government is obliged to give NCM at least two years' notice of its intention to withdraw its support.

Similar government support was extended to other private sector credit insurance companies. Special government-subsidised, short-term credit insurance is periodically made available for specified 'active' markets targeted in government export drives. Examples of active markets recently qualifying for preferential treatment are Egypt, Zimbabwe and Indonesia.

Apart from NCM, a number of other private sector companies offer export credit insurance (notably Trade Indemnity Ltd). Your usual insurance broker should be able to provide you with details. Private sector export credit insurers (including NCM) will provide their customers with both domestic and export credit under the terms of a single policy. They compete against each other in terms of such matters as:

- how quickly they deal with applications for cover;
- speed of settlement of claims;

- ability to tailor policies to clients' particular needs;
- the extent of the advice on export credit and financing matters that they provide, including the provision of credit ratings on potential customers;
- availability of 'catastrophe' policies – policies which, for a much reduced premium, cover only excessive levels of loss.

Types of cover

The most common type of cover is the *comprehensive policy* which indemnifies the exporter against *all* export credit risks involving transactions with a maximum six months' credit period. Policies operate continuously and last for one year at a time. Normally, cover begins the day goods are shipped, though for an extra premium a transaction can be covered from the day the contract is signed (up to a limit of 12 months between signing and shipment). Comprehensive cover offers guarantees against losses incurred through:

(a) insolvency of the foreign customer;
(b) failure of the customer to pay within six months for accepted goods;
(c) the customer's failure to accept goods already despatched, for reasons which are not the fault of the supplier, and where the insurer believes that legal action will not result in settlement;
(d) extra handling or transport charges owing to the necessary diversion of a consignment from its planned route, if these cannot be recovered from the buyer.

Insurers will not offer full indemnity to exporters, who must bear at least 15 per cent of losses caused by political factors, or 10 per cent of losses owing to commercial risk. Full indemnity might encourage firms to exercise insufficient care when choosing potential customers. You pay for comprehensive cover through either an annual premium or – if you are a small exporter whose foreign business is less than a certain amount – you can pay a single annual premium adjusted at a year's end to account for divergences between actual and anticipated sales. Typically, cover will cost between 0.5 and 1.5 per cent of the value of export sales depending on the spread of risk and the volume of your export work.

Specific cover is available from ECGD (and private insurers in appropriate circumstances) and relates to particular risks on long-term credit for projects involving major capital goods. A specific policy might be more expensive than comprehensive cover because

121

there is no spreading of risk. The ECGD also offers a variety of special policies, which alter periodically as circumstances change. Details are available from the ECGD head office. Since ECGD cover guarantees eventual payment, your bank may be willing to lend you money to finance that deal using the ECGD policy as security against your defaulting on payment.

For an extremely large transaction involving a major project, the ECGD may even help your customer to finance the deal. Under its Buyer Credit Scheme your customer pays you 15 to 20 per cent of the value of the sale on signature of the contract, the remainder being paid to you by a UK bank from a loan made by this bank to the customer. The UK bank's loan is guaranteed 100 per cent by the ECGD. You have to pay a premium to the ECGD to cover its guarantee to the bank, the cost of which you incorporate into your quoted price. The facility is only available on finance of at least £1 million extending over at least two years. The ECGD publishes a useful and informative brochure on the subject, *Buyer Credit: Flexible Finance for Project Exporters*, which you can obtain from them.

Similar to Buyer Credits are ECGD 'Lines of Credit', which cover many transactions and not just one. Lines of Credit can apply to individual contract values as low as £30,000–£50,000, although several contracts with unrelated buyers will normally be involved.

Applications and settlements

Export credit insurers clear around 80 per cent of applications for cover within 24 hours of receipt of an enquiry. You have to wait longer if a complex deal or a high degree of risk is involved. The timing of claims settlement varies by insurer and according to the cause of loss. The ECGD will settle as follows:

(a) Immediately on proof of the buyer's insolvency.
(b) Six months after the buyer has defaulted on accepted goods.
(c) One month after the resale of the goods if the original customer refuses to accept them and they have to be resold to third parties at a loss.
(d) Four months after the date of other causes of loss.

Private insurers offer comparable terms.

It is important to note that insurance cover against currency exchange risk is not available from either the ECGD or from private sources. See Chapter 6 for information on this matter.

Chapter 12
Legal Problems and Getting Paid

Bills of exchange, letters of credit and documentary collections are appropriate for situations in which foreign buyers place high value orders with the supplying firm, which may then protect itself against non-payment through discounting the bill of exchange or by taking out credit insurance with ECGD, NCM, Trade Indemnity, or some other credit insurance company (see Chapter 11). However, businesses that sell relatively low value items on credit direct to large numbers of foreign customers (with or without the use of agents) need to concern themselves with credit control and possibly the need to collect debts in foreign countries.

This is particularly true for sales to the European Union. Continental Europeans expect to pay for goods supplied from other EU countries using their own currency and on the same terms and conditions (including credit arrangements) as are available from local firms. Why otherwise should they bother to buy from a foreign business, considering the widespread availability of credit and the extensive range of high quality products offered to them by competing companies? European customers are not interested in bills of exchange, letters of credit or any of the other paraphernalia connected with non-EU international trade.

In 1994, over 85 per cent of cross-border EU transactions were settled by cheque, and the figure is increasing. Thus, firms must be prepared to quote local currency prices, accept local cheques as payment, and offer whatever credit is customary in the country concerned.

Unfortunately, the increase in the volume of intra-EU commercial transactions brought about by the completion of the Single Market has been accompanied by a corresponding rise in the magnitude of outstanding cross-border debt! Economic recession in some EU nations and slowdowns in others have caused significant expansions in the average periods for which commercial debts are outstanding in all EU states. Even firms in nations which in the past had good reputations for prompt settlement (Denmark and Germany, for instance)

GETTING STARTED IN EXPORT

now seem to have acquired the habit of delaying settlement of bills. Nevertheless, credit is a critically important marketing device and, as the pan-European market develops, firms are sure to compete fiercely by offering increasingly attractive credit terms.

Certain EU countries are noted for their exceptionally long standard credit periods. Belgian firms, for instance, do not regard 120-day credit terms as unusual (90 days is the norm), and substantial discounts will be demanded for early settlement of bills (possibly 2½ per cent for payment within ten days). Ninety- to 120-day credit is also common in Portugal and Spain, sometimes longer.

In Italy there is a major difference between consumer goods buyers and industrial goods buyers where credit is concerned. Italian consumers still pay by cash or cheque for the great majority of items, so that protracted customer credit is rare. Italian industrial buyers, however, demand extremely long settlement periods, up to seven months on occasion. The Netherlands is another country with a cash payment tradition, and settlement terms of anything exceeding 14 to 30 days are uncommon for consumer purchases. The Irish are accustomed to end of month payment.

Question. How can I avoid having to collect debts owed by foreign customers to whom I have sold on credit?
Answer. Use the services of a credit factoring company.

Factoring services

Factoring involves the sale of export invoices to a credit factor in exchange for a cash payment (typically 75 to 80 per cent of the face value of invoices in the first instance, the remainder when customers settle their outstanding accounts). The factoring company then assumes full responsibility for collecting the money.

A variation on this is 'invoice discounting' whereby the supplier receives a cash payment (effectively a loan) from the invoice discounter against the value of the invoices issued to customers, but retains responsibility for debt collection and for an agreed proportion of bad debt.

'Captive factoring' occurs where large industrial groups establish their own factoring subsidiaries which offer factoring services to all suppliers of the parent firm.

Factors are expert in the laws and techniques of international debt collection. Usually, they operate through international networks of credit factors, providing reciprocal services for fellow members.

These networks enable factors in various countries to communicate with customers in the latter's own languages and to apply collection procedures appropriate to the country concerned. Thus, local telephone calls can be made to remind customers to settle overdue accounts, local legal representation can be arranged quickly in order to pursue recalcitrant debtors, and so on.

Factoring is most common in Italy (due to restrictions on bank lending imposed in the early 1990s), followed by the USA and the UK. Despite possessing the largest economy in Europe, Germany has Europe's lowest factoring turnover – largely because of the law on the 'Prohibition of Assignment' which allows buyers contractually to prohibit suppliers from assigning their invoices to third parties. Also, reservation of title clauses (see pages 127–8) are easier to impose in Germany than elsewhere.

How much will it cost?

This depends on the riskiness of the transaction and the extent of the paperwork involved. Typically, there is a service charge of 1 to 2 per cent of the value of sales (to cover the cost of administration), a 'financing charge' (equivalent to loan interest) on the money released by the factor, plus a premium of about 1 per cent of sales (to cover the cost of dealing with bad debts). The financing charge will normally be 3 to 5 per cent above bank base rate and is payable on the period between your receipt of cash from the factor and the dates that creditors settle their bills.

If you invoice DDP (delivered duty paid) in local foreign currency, you can usually elect to have the residual 20 to 25 per cent of your total payment in the relevant local currency. This can reduce the financing charge because interest rates in many countries are far lower than in the UK, and the effects of these lower rates are passed back to the client.

In addition to these charges you might have to pay any legal fees incurred by the factor while collecting money owed against your invoices, according to the terms of your agreement. If the customer ultimately defaults, the factor may or may not be able to reclaim part of the loss from you, depending on the precise terms of your contract. However, 100 per cent bad debt protection is available from most factors on payment of an additional premium.

Increasingly, factors offer ancillary services to their clients, such as information on customers; industry norms for prices and terms and conditions of sale; news about which regions and industries are experiencing recession (evidenced by exceptionally late payment by firms in these industries and regions) and so on. The large factoring companies provide this information via on-line computer viewdata facilities available on a monthly, weekly or even daily basis.

Finding a factor

Most of the large UK banks provide factoring services, and numerous UK credit factoring companies undertake foreign work. The Association of British Factors will provide lists of its members currently active in various foreign markets. When selecting a factor look carefully at how the firm operates – does it guarantee to take all your invoices or just some of them, and how quickly will you receive the cash? You need to compare both the terms of various factors and indeed the costs of factoring with the benefits of not having to collect your own debts. Depending on circumstances, the following questions might be relevant to your choice of factor:

- How will customers react to having to pay their debts to a factor rather than yourself?
- If the factor 'lends' you money against the security of invoices, will this affect your relationships with other lenders (particularly your bank) who might regard outstanding debtors as an important constituent part of the security you offer against loans?
- Is the factor willing to disclose the names and addresses of other clients whom you can approach for a reference?

The problems involved

Factoring and invoice discounting, while convenient, can be expensive compared to the interest payable on loans. Also, the client company is usually expected to sign a 12-month agreement with the factor or discounter so that it becomes locked into using factoring/discounting services. Another issue is the effect on customer relations of using a factoring company, which will pursue outstanding debts vigorously, regardless of possible damaging effects on the client's business image.

Debt collecting in foreign countries

The costs and other problems of factoring lead some firms to collect on their own invoices and independently seek to recover long outstanding debts. This might be appropriate where the risks of non-payment are small and/or where the effects on the supplying firm of eventual non-payment by certain foreign customers will not be excessively damaging.

It is important to realise, however, that debt collecting in foreign countries is troublesome, time-consuming and can be very expensive. Foreign lawyers must be engaged; procedures are lengthy and outcomes uncertain. Thus, it is essential to conduct proper credit rating checks on potential customers. All the major banks offer credit rating services. References may also be obtained from national credit agencies (contact points for which are available via local Chambers of Commerce) and/or from international credit management organisations (Dun and Bradstreet, for example).

Yet, no matter how carefully you check out the credit worthiness of prospective clients in other states, collection difficulties will inevitably arise and be exacerbated by the fact that the debts have to be collected abroad. Among the special difficulties associated with foreign debt collecting are:

- the need to conduct correspondence and/or make telephone calls in a foreign language;
- not being able conveniently to visit the customer in order to discuss the debt;
- not knowing the whereabouts and facilities of local collection agencies;
- unfamiliarity with the legal debt collection and insolvency rules of the country concerned.

Collecting bills of exchange
If a bill of exchange is involved in an export transaction, the buyer defaults and it is your responsibility to collect the money, then the first step towards recovery through local courts is to have the bill protested. This means getting a notary public (a local person legally qualified to attest and clarify documents) to ask the customer for payment or reasons for non-payment. The information is put into a formal deed of protest which your solicitor then places before a local court as evidence of dishonour. It may be that even if you have taken out payments insurance in respect of a bill of exchange you will still be expected to attempt to obtain the outstanding amount by taking legal action in the foreign country prior to registering a claim against your insurance.

Reservation of title
It is possible to incorporate into your standard contract of sale a 'reservation of title' (RT) clause (sometimes called a *Romalpa* clause after the court case that established the precedent in these respects)

127

whereby goods supplied to the customer remain the property of the supplying firm until they are paid for. Thus, should the customer sell the goods to a third party before reneging on the debt, the supplier can approach the third party and reclaim the items, which in law still belong to the supplier.

This is not a straightforward matter. The circumstances in which international courts will accept the legitimacy of such contracts are complex and you must consult a solicitor before attempting such a sale. However, the possibility is perhaps worth investigating if your output is high value and of such a nature that its reclamation from customers in a resaleable condition is practicable.

There are two types of RT clause: *simple* and *extended*. The former occurs in the circumstances already outlined, such as where the seller retains ownership until cash payment is received or a cheque is cleared. More difficult are extended RT clauses, which come in two varieties.

1. The buyer is regarded as an agent of the supplier and, if the goods are sold to a third party, the money received is viewed as being 'held in trust' on the supplier's behalf. Thus, should the first buyer become insolvent before paying the supplier, the latter has a claim on that firm's assets even to the point of being able to reclaim the goods in question from the third (or subsequent) parties to whom they were resold.

2. The clause may state that if the goods supplied are used as inputs (for example, as raw materials) to other goods, the original supplier retains a financial interest in the final goods that result, unless the final goods possess a different 'commercial identity' from the original goods' input. For example, a supplier of leather to a handbag manufacturer was held not to have title to handbags sold to the public by the manufacturer, despite the existence of an extended RT clause.

Foreign legal systems

Fortunately, there are many similarities in the legal systems of many of the world's major trading nations due in part to the 1804 French Code Napoleon, which was subsequently imposed on Belgium, Italy, Luxembourg, the Netherlands, Spain, Greece, Portugal and regions of Germany (Westphalia, Baden and the Rhineland) occupied by France during the Napoleonic Wars. This system was subsequently transmitted outside Europe to other regions colonised by some of these countries. The other major systems are (a) the common law system found in the UK, the USA and Canada, Australia and parts of Africa previously colonised by the British, and (b) the Islamic system.

Under the common law system, legal rulings depend on historical precedent, specific cases and ad-hoc legislation. In countries with a legal code all laws are written down and either the Criminal Code, Civil Code or Commercial Code used to determine all legal matters.

Islamic law is not fundamentally dissimilar to common law or code law approaches where business is concerned. Note, moreover, that many Islamic countries are ex-colonies or protectorates of western nations so that elements of the legal system of the ex-colonial power strongly influence the way that Islamic laws (taken from the Koran) are interpreted and applied.

Nevertheless, exporters need to be aware of the extent to which commercial laws can differ among nations. Important disparities among the legal systems of various countries include the following:

1. The intervals beyond which cases become 'statute barred' (so that no one can sue for compensation) differ among states. In Britain, the period for most classes of contract is six years; in France it can be up to 30 years; in Germany it depends on whether the case concerns a commercial transaction and, if so, whether both parties to the contract are business firms.

2. Laws concerning the circumstances in which an offer may be withdrawn without penalty vary in detail between nations. Normally, the law of the country in which obligations arising from a contract are performed will apply to such matters, although many disputes arise over the question of where exactly the performance was intended to take place.

3. Consideration does not necessarily have to be proven prior to suing for breach of contract in certain countries. Examples of 'consideration' are the price paid for goods, the wages of employees (as consideration for providing labour), the hire fee paid for the lease of equipment, etc. Under English law a contract cannot exist without consideration.

4. National differences occur *vis-à-vis* the legality of exemption clauses and penalty clauses incorporated into contracts.

5. In some countries there is a legal distinction between people who perform commercial acts ('traders') and other citizens. Different rules regarding what is and is not a contract might appertain to traders; legal disputes involving traders may be heard in 'commercial courts' separate from the rest of the country's legal

system; and different rules on bankruptcy could apply. A higher standard of commercial responsibility may be expected of a trader, and penalties for breach of contract, fraud, etc might be heavier than for ordinary members of the public. Conversely, proceedings are faster, cheaper and less formal in a commercial court than in the rest of the country's legal system and the rules of evidence might be less severe. Also, the extent of the proof needed to establish the existence of a contract could be less than for cases involving private persons.

Resolution of disputes with customers

As soon as your goods enter foreign territory they become subject to foreign laws concerning technical standards, safety, liability for defects, packaging and labelling, brand names, length of guarantees, pricing and promotion, etc. International legal considerations also affect the ways in which contracts of sale are drafted, the carriage of goods, insurance of payments and of consignments, and the means of financing deals.

If you are unfortunate enough to have a serious dispute with a foreign customer, distributor, advertising agent, etc, the matter will have to be resolved, ultimately, through the courts. Legal action occurs *in the country of the party that is being sued*. Thus, for example, a UK exporter alleging breach of contract by a Taiwanese customer must instigate legal proceedings in Taiwan. If the contract of sale specified that the laws of England would apply to the deal then the Taiwanese court hearing the case would have to interpret the contract according to *English* rather than Taiwanese law, leading to great complexity and many delays. Also, of course, different laws, interpretations and legal methods apply to commercial litigation within each nation, and conflicts between the legal system of specific countries commonly occur.

International conventions

A number of international agreements govern the legal frameworks to be applied to particular aspects of cross-border trade. Jurisdictional issues within the European Union, for example, are covered by the Brussels Convention of 1982 and the Rome Convention of 1990, which establish the (sometimes complex) circumstances in which cases will be heard in particular EU nations.

If the contract of sale does not name a country, then the courts of the country with 'the closest connection' with the contract will handle the case. Laws concerning *the carriage of goods at sea* follow the 'Hague–Visby Rules' in the majority of the world's trading nations. Notwithstanding this fact, nearly all bills of lading (see Chapter 9) include clauses explicitly stating that a least some of the Hague–Visby rules will apply.

The 'Hague Rules' were drafted in 1921 and subsequently extended (to become the Hague–Visby Rules) via the 1968 Brussels Protocol. Hague–Visby Rules formally determine the legal status of the bill of lading and specify upper limits and a formula for calculating the carrier's liability for damage to cargoes. Claims must be lodged within one year of delivery or the date a cargo was lost.

Air transport is covered by the Warsaw Convention of 1929 (subsequently amended) which sets maximum limits on liability for negligence and regulates the legal relationships between air carriers and consignees. Conditions and performance of contracts for *rail transport* are governed by the 1985 *Convention Relative aux Transports Internationaux Ferroviares* (COTIF).

European road haulage is governed by the 1956 *Convention de Marchandises par Route* (CMR Convention) which lays down standard international contractual conditions for road transport, covering liability for loss or damage to goods and the maximum value for insurance claims against the haulier. Under the Convention the carrier is fully responsible for the acts and omissions of employees and agents, and specific documentation must be used. The Convention extends to contracts involving 'successive carriers', such as road, rail, sea and air.

Two international Conventions have sought to harmonise the legal rules concerning the *international sale of goods*. The Hague Convention of 1964 drafted 'Uniform Laws' for (a) the sale of goods across national frontiers, and (b) the formation of contracts for international sales. These Uniform Laws were reconsidered, extended and developed by the United Nations Commission on International Trade Law (UNCITRAL), which organised a 'Vienna Convention' to draft a commercial code for use in all international transactions. The resulting code included a clearly defined procedure for arbitration. The intention of the Hague and Vienna Conventions was that agreed Uniform Laws be incorporated into the domestic law of all United Nations countries. This has indeed occurred in many states, including the USA, France, Italy, the Netherlands and Scandinavia. In countries that have not acceded to the Convention (Britain, for example) the Uniform Laws apply only if both parties agree to this happening.

Intellectual property

A number of international Conventions and agreements have been concluded to provide residents of member countries with intellectual property protection in other states. The main ones are:

- the Madrid Agreement of 1988 whereby the holder of a trade mark may register it with the World Intellectual Property Organisation (WIPO) in Geneva to extend cover to about 30 countries worldwide. WIPO circulates the trade mark to all countries that have signed the Madrid Agreement, where it is processed according to local intellectual property laws. The applicant then receives a bundle of national trade mark registrations;

- the Paris Convention for the Protection of Industrial Property, signed by 90 countries. Members are obliged to recognise all intellectual property rights over patents, trade marks, etc held by residents of other member nations. Hence, each member country must afford the same degree of protection over intellectual property to nationals of other member states as it gives to its own citizens. Someone registering a trade mark in one country has up to six months' grace prior to having to register in another (12 months for patents), and the owner's rights over the intellectual property are automatically maintained during this period;

- the Inter-American Convention of the USA and most Latin American countries. This provides protection essentially similar to that afforded by the Paris Convention;

- the European Patent Convention which makes it possible to obtain patent protection throughout the European Union with a single application (made through the inventor's own national patent office). The 'exhaustion of rights' doctrine applies to all EU patents, no matter where they are registered. This means that a patent holder of a product patented in any one EU country cannot prohibit its sale in others, in other words, the patent holder has no right to prevent the export of the patented item to other EU nations.

Arbitration

The commonest procedures for resolving disputes involving the conflict of national laws are (a) to specify explicitly in the initial contract that the law of a particular nation shall apply to the deal, or (b) to insert an arbitration clause into the contract under which an international body will resolve the issue. The United Nations Commission on International Trade Law (UNCITRAL) does not *itself* provide arbitration facilities; rather, it lays down a model set of rules and procedures which other bodies (the International Chamber of Commerce [ICC], the American Arbitration Association, the London Court of Arbitration or the International Centre for Settlement of Investment Disputes, for example) can apply to their deliberations.

The ICC is the most commonly used arbitration organisation. It is based in Paris and offers arbitration facilities both to member and non-member companies. ICC proceedings begin with an attempt at conciliation by a panel of three persons nominated by the President of the ICC, followed by the appointment of an arbitration tribunal whose members are nationals of countries not involved in the dispute.

If the parties to a contract agree to arbitration then the arbitrator's decision becomes legally binding under their domestic laws via the 1958 New York Convention on the Recognition and Enforcement of Foreign Arbitral Awards, the rules of which the overwhelming majority of the world's country's have accepted.

Exchange controls

Although totally absent in the European Union, some countries (notably the poorer, underdeveloped nations) occasionally resort to the use of exchange controls in order to protect their balance of payments situations. Exchange controls restrict importers' abilities to obtain the foreign currency needed to pay for imports. Controls operate either via direct prohibition or through the government artificially increasing the exchange rate prices of certain foreign currencies (possibly by limiting the supply of these currencies available for importers to purchase).

Administration of exchange controls is complex and problematic for the authorities of the country in question and may involve:

- legal requirements that firms hand over to the national central bank all the foreign exchange they acquire;
- government rules that different exchange rates apply to different types of transaction (although this is extremely rare under a long-standing international agreement that prohibits the use of multiple exchange rates for normal import/export activity);
- restriction of foreign exchange availability to the import of certain specified products;
- selection of particular firms that may obtain foreign exchange;
- imposition of foreign exchange queues and waiting lists;

- only allowing foreign exchange to importers who enter into joint venture, domestic manufacturing arrangements with exporting companies.

To the extent that exchange control problems create significant risks of non-payment, you need to ensure that your payments insurance includes adequate cover against the possibility of the foreign government declaring a moratorium on the release of foreign exchange to pay for imports. Alternatively, you could factor your invoices (see pages 124–5) or insist on a confirmed irrevocable letter of credit. In the former case, however, the factor's discount will be very high for risky countries, while in the latter a UK bank will not add its confirmation to any letter of credit issued by a bank in a country from which the UK bank believes it will be difficult to extract payment.

In general, the poorer the country the more likely it is to place restrictions on the availability to domestic residents of the foreign currency needed to pay for imports. Typical procedures are as follows:

1. All imports have to be registered with the central bank of the importing country.
2. Importers have to apply for licences to enable them to purchase, at a prespecified rate, foreign exchange that will be paid to foreign exporters.
3. Exporters must submit pro-forma invoices to their customers in the importing country.
4. Shipments are subject to inspections to verify that the price of the goods matches their level of quality and that only the quantity actually shipped is being paid for (not a greater amount).

Licences themselves may be allocated according to government discretion or auctioned. Foreign exchange might only be available to importers of certain categories of item (luxury consumer goods, for example) at very expensive rates.

Countertrade
This means the direct or indirect exchange of goods for other goods across national frontiers. It is found in situations where one or more of the parties is unable to pay for imports using foreign currency, either because its central bank has insufficient stocks of foreign exchange or in conseqence of government restrictions on the availability of foreign exchange imposed for political reasons.

As someone new to exporting you will not be concerned with countertrade in the early stages of your international operations.

However, it is important to understand the extent of countertrading in world markets and to be prepared to engage in it as your experience of international trading increases. According to the OECD, countertrade may account for anything up to 5 per cent of total world trade, 10 per cent for trade involving developing nations, and 35 per cent for trade between the latter and East European states.

Countertrade can be used by exporters to offer what are, in effect, extremely favourable 'prices' to potential customers in countries where there is fierce local competition. Indeed, a customer in a country where there are *no* foreign exchange controls or shortages may well – confronted by two competing offers from foreign exporting firms, one involving countertrade and the other demanding cash – choose the deal with countertrade.

Countertrade intermediaries will store and process goods and advertise and otherwise promote the item on offer. The intermediary will act either as an agent or a principal, charging between 3 and 15 per cent commission for its services. Today, the countertrade industry is worldwide, with firms operating in all major trading capitals (in the past, most countertrade was organised through Vienna and London).

Types of countertrade transaction

The simplest form of countertrade is *barter*, otherwise known as *contratrading* or *reciprocal trading*. A situation wherein the exporter (or an intermediary) arranges for the disposal of the barter goods to a third party is called a 'switch deal'.

Compensation dealing is where the exporting firm receives part payment in its own currency and the remainder in goods. *Buyback* arises when a firm supplies plant and equipment to a foreign importer under a contract requiring the exporter to accept output produced by the plant and equipment supplied as a whole or part payment for the transaction. Sometimes a government will sanction the import of major capital goods only on condition that they contain a specified proportion of local inputs or that the exporter agrees to purchase locally produced items of at least a certain value. This is known as an 'offset' arrangement and might include a buyback element.

With a *counterpurchase* arrangement the exporting firm receives part payment in its own currency or a hard foreign currency (one that is freely exchangeable in any other currency) and the balance in the currency of the importer's country. The exporter then uses the latter currency to buy whatever products happen to be available in the importer's country.

Chapter 13
An Export Plan

As soon as you decide to take exporting seriously, you need to prepare an export plan. The purpose of such a plan is threefold:

1. to compel you and your colleagues to examine the merits and demerits of exporting critically, objectively and systematically;
2. to generate commitment to exporting among the staff who will be involved in implementing the process;
3. to establish priorities and to relate exporting to your overall business strategies.

A good way to set about writing the plan is to ask yourself and then answer a number of critical questions, as outlined below. Not all the questions will be relevant to your particular firm, though most have a common application. The plan itself should be prepared under the following headings:

1. Reasons for exporting
● What gave you the idea of exporting in the first instance?
● How do you anticipate that exporting will benefit your firm?
● How will exporting fit in with your overall business strategies?

2. Marketing
(a) Market entry
● What criteria have you adopted for selecting the foreign markets in which you intend doing business, and what is your rationale for using these criteria?
● Have you identified any barriers that could prevent you from entering target markets and, if so, how will these be overcome?
● Will you be using foreign agents? If so, how will potential agents be found?
● Is it possible to use direct marketing for your intended foreign sales?

- What are the levels of import tariff and/or local taxes in each intended foreign market?
- How will you redraft existing sales literature to make it suitable for reuse in other countries?

(b) Resources

- Are you fully satisfied with your existing marketing arrangements here in the UK? If not, how can you justify seeking to extend your sales efforts to include foreign countries?
- How can weaknesses in the firm's present marketing activities be remedied?
- What resource constraints are likely to restrict future export marketing developments? Can anything be done to remove these limiting factors?
- How much of the work attached to export marketing can be completed in-house and how much will have to be subcontracted?

(c) Nature of intended markets

- What are the key characteristics of the types of foreign customer most likely to buy your product?
- Which market segments offer the best chances of success? Why will foreign buyers wish to purchase your goods?
- How will foreign customers get to know about your products? Will you need to advertise and, if so, in which media and to what extent?
- How will customers be able to place orders for your goods?

(d) Pricing

- What are the maximum price levels that each target market will bear?
- What mark-ups on your domestic UK prices will be necessary to cover all the costs of exporting that you will have to incur?
- Are there any legally binding price controls in your intended foreign markets? If so, what are their implications for your export marketing effort?
- What pricing strategies are available to you in each foreign market?
- Do you expect foreign customers to change their levels of consumption of the product by large amounts following small price alterations?

(e) Market research

- How much research into target foreign markets have you already undertaken?
- Are local market research companies available in the various countries in which you intend doing business?
- What information gathering systems will you install in order to monitor developments in foreign markets?

3. Supply

(a) The product(s) to be offered

- What are the unique selling points of your product offer compared to those of products supplied by rival foreign companies?
- To what extent will it be necessary to redesign your products to make them appeal to wider international markets? If extensive redesign is needed, who will complete this work, how and when?
- Have you identified all the foreign technical standards relevant to your output? How will you amend your production and quality assurance processes to ensure that outputs comply with foreign technical standards?
- What changes in your standard warranty agreements and periods will be necessary in order to sell in target foreign markets?
- How will you provide adequate after-sales service and customer care facilities in foreign countries?

(b) Resources

- Is the firm's product range adequate for export marketing?
- Do you have sufficient production and flexibility to be able to satisfy additional export orders?
- Does the design and product development function command sufficient status within your firm, considering the importance of this for export marketing?
- What are the core technologies most likely to influence the product offers of your own business and of competing firms over the next few years?

4. Competition

- What are the competitive situations in various foreign markets in terms of:
  - extent of competition;
  - competitors' strengths and weaknesses;

- government controls on business activity (price and import controls, laws and regulations on selling methods, etc)?
- How likely is it that fresh competitors will enter the market?
- What are the critical success factors that seemingly determine which firms do well when selling your category of product in each target market? What are the sources of competitive advantage for successful firms? What marketing strategies have successful businesses adopted?

5. Export organisation

- Who is to be in charge of export operations and what is your rationale for appointing this person?
- How is the export department to be structured?
- Where are the additional resources needed to support the export function to come from? How will administrative support for the export department be organised?
- What status will the people concerned with exporting command within the organisation?
- How will the export department fit in with the firm's wider organisational structure? How will export personnel relate to managers in other parts of the business?

6. Staffing

- What technical and managerial skills will staff need to acquire in order to sell to foreign markets?
- How much will it cost to train staff in relevant export competencies?
- To what extent will it be necessary to engage outside consultants? How much will consultancy assistance cost and how will consultants relate to in-house employees?
- Are existing staff motivated towards achieving export objectives and culturally attuned to the requirements of export work? If not, how are you going to instil enthusiasm for exporting among key employees?
- If you intend recruiting fresh staff to handle the firm's export activities, where will they come from and how much will they cost?

7. Transport and distribution

- Have you examined all the transport options available and related them to customer requirements? What are the costs and benefits of each alternative?

- What special distribution problems apply to your products (breakages, perishability of output, need for expensive packaging, possibility of contamination, etc) and how will they be overcome?

- What measures can be taken to prevent pilfering while the goods are *en route*?

- What are the warehousing requirements for your consignments? Have you identified the best possible locations for warehousing your goods?

- To what extent are local intermediaries available to help with distribution and how much will they cost?

8. Financial aspects

- Have you estimated your export start-up costs?
- How will your export financing requirements be met?
- How are you going to allocate overheads to the export function?
- What are your cash-flow forecasts in relation to exports?
- Have you computed break-even points for export sales?
- Can your existing credit control system cope with the possible need to collect debts in foreign countries? If you decide to use the services of a factoring company, how much will this cost?

- Will your costing system enable you to establish the variable costs of exported output and the contributions of exports to total profits?

- What yardsticks will you use for monitoring export performance? How do you justify your choice of criteria for measuring performance?

9. Contingency plans

- What are your key export objectives and what will you do if any one of them is not met within a specific period?

- What will happen if foreign distribution is disrupted? What alternative distribution methods can be used at short notice if your intended distribution channels are not available?

- Have you calculated the full costs of consignment and payments insurance?

Chapter 14

Selling to Western Europe

The European Union is the largest and most affluent single market in the developed world, with around 375 million potential customers. Business laws and practices have been (or are being) harmonised across the entire region, and there is free movement of goods, persons and capital.

Of particular importance is the so-called 'Golden Triangle' (see Figure 14.1). This encompasses all or parts of the UK, Belgium, France, Germany, Luxembourg and the Netherlands (with end points around Liverpool, Paris and Hamburg) and which, despite having a land mass smaller than the United Kingdom, is home to 60 per cent of the EU's population and offers businesses a consumer market equal in value to 80 per cent of that of the USA.

All locations within the Golden Triangle are within a day's drive from any starting point. Income per capita is among the highest in the world, and there is much lucrative business for any firm offering attractive products at the right quality and the right price. Within the Triangle itself (and increasingly within Western Europe as a whole) consumers have similar tastes, buying habits, lifestyles and requirements in relation to the quality of products: they want goods that are novel, appealing and, above all, reliable and of the highest quality.

Nature of the West European market

There are four really large markets in Western Europe: Germany (population about 80 million), France (57 million), Italy (58 million) and the UK (58 million). The dominant demographic fact about the EU is the low (or zero) rate of population growth in most of its member nations. This has caused a significant rise in the average age of West Europeans and, in consequence, changing attitudes and spending patterns among European consumers. All EU countries are well-off compared to the majority of the world's nations, and even the poorer members are experiencing steady, long-term, economic growth. Importantly, moreover, all the lower income Union countries

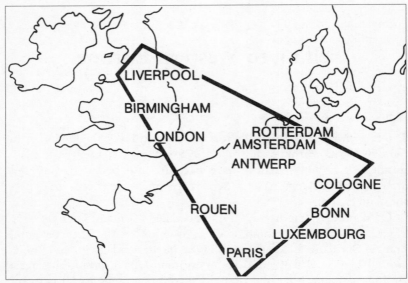

Figure 14.1 *The 'Golden Triangle'*
Source: Butterworths, 1983

contain substantial groups of consumers whose tastes, living standards and lifestyles are virtually identical to those of equivalent consumers in the richer EU states.

Harmonisation of business practices

Decisions taken at the EU level pass into Union law (which is binding on all member states) through one of the following devices:

(a) *Regulations* or laws that apply immediately and equally in all member states.
(b) *Directives*, which specify a necessary outcome (such as to prevent misleading advertising) but then allow the government of each member country to introduce its own particular legislation to achieve the desired objective.
(c) *Decisions* of the European Court of Justice, which have the same effect as Regulations.

Additionally, the European Commission issues *Recommendations* which are not legally binding, but express the Commission's considered opinions about how certain matters should be dealt with.

Today, EU Directives, Regulations, etc affect most aspects of European business. There are Directives on consumer protection, advertising and cross-border broadcasting, company administration, intellectual property, agency and distribution arrangements, business mergers and acquisitions, working conditions, health and safety, gender equal opportunities in employment, and on numerous other facets of business life. Some of these EU Directives are even being adopted by a number of non-EU states.

Post-Second World War Western Europe has seen the emergence of comparable fashions, music, television programmes and, importantly, a broadly similar youth culture in all industrially developed nations. The fact that more Europeans visit other countries than at any time in history has greatly contributed to this trend, as have the activities of large, multinational companies that offer near identical products in all European states. However, European economic integration does *not* mean that Germans will cease to be German, that the Dutch will no longer be Dutch, or that the French will not be French. The Single Market has in no way created 'grey uniformity' among national consumer populations. Indeed, regional cultures appear, if anything, to have been reinforced, with the consequence that small but significant niche markets are flourishing throughout the Union.

The proposed single currency

The common European currency is scheduled for introduction to the EU's core economies by the end of the decade. Britain and Denmark have negotiated opt-out clauses but, even without their participation, the creation of a single currency (initially within France, Germany and Benelux perhaps) will alter fundamentally and forever the extent and pattern of European trade. It will require firms to quote prices in a common unit and will enable consumers readily to compare the prices of similar items sold in various EU countries.

A common currency means pan-European price labelling and packaging, easier product positioning in national markets, and the absence of currency conversion costs for businesses in nations that are members of the scheme. Firms outside the common currency area, conversely, will need separate prices, packaging and labelling for domestic and European markets, and must incur the substantial expense of currency conversion.

A common currency removes *entirely* the currency exchange risk associated with international transactions. However, such risks – and the consequent need to hedge against them via the forward currency exchange markets – will continue to apply to non-common currency area enterprises. A major advantage will be the clearer and better information made available on input costs and competitors' prices. The assessment of potential customers' creditworthiness should be facilitated.

Why export to Western Europe?

West European integration presents numerous opportunities for the individual firm. The compulsory application of EU-wide technical product standards enables small enterprises to compete in all EU states, and public sector contracts across the entire Union are now open to tender by any EU business (subject to certain minimum threshold values – see public procurement, pages 147–8). Minimal documentation is required when transporting goods across national EU frontiers and there are no customs duties as such (but see VAT on EU exports, page 107). You declare your foreign EU sales in your normal VAT returns.

Specific reasons for selling to Continental EU nations include the following:

- Considerable market research information is available on West European countries and is easily assessed.
- You do not have to worry about quota restrictions or other non-tariff barriers to trade.
- Continental West European markets are highly stable.
- Consumers in many EU countries are much wealthier than in the UK.
- There are already large numbers of UK businesses selling to each of the EU nations and you can approach these firms for advice and assistance (through a Chamber of Commerce, the commercial departments of British Diplomatic Posts, your own UK bank, etc) when entering the market.
- A strong demand for good quality British products continues to exist among Continental EU consumers.
- You can travel to all parts of Western Europe quickly and conveniently if problems requiring immediate attention arise unexpectedly.
- As Continental EU languages are widely taught in British schools and colleges it is not difficult to find translators of standard com-

mercial documents, advertisements, etc from English into these
languages.

- The Continent has an excellent and wide-ranging rail network
  that can be used for onward distribution of products throughout
  Eastern Europe and beyond.
- Continental EU attitudes towards business are not dissimilar to
  those in the UK.

Succeeding in EU markets

Successful selling in West European countries requires that you project sound and concrete images of high quality products, that wher-
ever possible you enable Continental customers to obtain your goods
direct from a local supply point (such as a retail outlet) rather than
having to order them from an address in Britain, and that you allow
customers to pay in their own local currency and on the same terms
and conditions (including credit terms) available from local suppliers.

Normally, it is best either to conceal the UK origin of your products – by marketing them under a local language name and using
quintessentially local promotional images – or to identify them as
undeniably British, playing on traditional Continental perceptions of
what the British are like, and using plenty of highly stereotyped
English (or Scottish) characterisations.

On balance, it is perhaps rather more difficult for British goods to
be sold simply under a 'Made in Britain' label in view of past difficulties concerning supply problems (real or imaginary) with UK firms:
late deliveries, inadequate after-sales service, communication break-
downs, and so on.

Test marketing

Without doubt, Belgium is one of the best places to test market a new
product in order to ascertain its suitability for Western Europe as a
whole. The country is multilingual and spans two cultures – the
Flemish-speaking people of the North and the French speakers of the
South – thus representing in miniature the essential characteristics of
Western Europe as a whole. The structure of consumption in terms
of the percentages of total income spent on food, clothes, furniture,
health products, rent, leisure goods, etc is very close to the average
for Western Europe as a whole, as are figures for the age structure of
the population, household size, earnings from various categories of

employment, and many other key indicators of interest to firms wishing to sell to the Continental EU.

Advertising in the European Union

International advertising generally is discussed in Chapter 8. Exporters new to Continental European advertising frequently fail to realise the substantial differences that exist between British and Continental advertising practices and laws. Note that to date there has been significantly more advertising in the UK than elsewhere in Europe (about 2 per cent of UK gross national product is devoted to advertising – more than in any other EU country). Consequently, the UK advertising industry is bigger than in Continental nations, with many more agencies, copywriters, media independents, public relations consultants, and so on. Advertising is completely integrated into UK culture and is accepted by UK consumers as a matter of course. This is not always the case in the rest of the European Union.

Past legislative constraints on media availability (prohibitions on television advertising or commercial radio, for example) in certain EU countries have caused the same product to be advertised in different media in different states – newspapers in one country, trade magazines in another, commercial radio in a third, etc. Also, copywriting, typesetting and printing costs differ markedly across European countries.

There is an EU Directive to prohibit misleading advertising. The latter is defined as advertising that deceives or is likely to deceive the people it reaches and which, by virtue of its deceptive nature, could affect consumer behaviour or cause damage to a competing firm. The EU insists, moreover, that (a) the burden of proof should lie with the advertiser and not with the consumer, and (b) national courts shall be empowered to halt the publication of misleading advertising. Moves are afoot, moreover, to introduce binding Directives in the following areas:

(a) Banning advertisements aimed at children which exploit either their inexperience or credulity, or their trust in teachers or parents.
(b) Controlling the ways in which women are portrayed in advertisements.
(c) Prohibiting motor car advertisements that feature speed and acceleration as primary selling points.

(d) Insisting that pharmaceuticals be advertised as medicines and not as foodstuffs or 'health products'.
(e) Heavily restricting all forms of alcohol advertising.
(f) Restricting the nature of the claims made when advertising food products, notably assertions that a food product provides nutrition not available in a normal diet, or is pure, new, additive free, natural or superior to others.

Additionally, the European Commission wants to see the establishment of low-cost legal procedures for consumers seeking compensation for minor damage caused by product inadequacy, and laws requiring that guarantees are honoured in EU consumers' countries of residence, regardless of where the product was purchased.

Public procurement

The public sector is an important customer for many European companies. Completion of the Single Market has been accompanied by the opening up of public sector contracts to competitive bidding by any EU firm irrespective of its geographical location. It is intended that within a few years, *all* public procurement will be subject to competitive tendering. Meanwhile, however, certain restrictions continue.

At the time of writing, there are three types of tendering procedure (open, restricted and negotiated) available for use by EU public bodies. *Open* tendering means that *any* company may enter a bid. *Restricted* tendering requires bidding companies to satisfy certain prequalifications set by the purchaser (such as providing evidence of their technical expertise and/or financial standing). *Negotiated* procedures relate to direct discussions between the purchaser and chosen suppliers, without any competition. This may only occur (a) if no tenders have been received using the other procedures; or (b) in consequence of the highly technical nature of the goods (for example, the need for compatibility with existing stocks); or (c) for reasons of extreme urgency. Purchasers can be forced to justify a decision to use negotiated procedures to the European Commission. Only contracts with values exceeding certain thresholds are covered by the legislation, as follows:

(a) For 'supplies contracts' (those involving the provision of goods to central, regional and local government and similar bodies such as police forces, local health authorities etc), the lower limits are 200,000 ECU (currently about £140,000) for regional and local government, or 130,000 ECU for central government.

(b) For 'works contracts' (building and civil engineering projects for central, regional and local government and similar bodies), only contracts worth more than 5 million ECU are covered.

Public purchasers must specify in advance the criteria (price, quality, etc) to be used in awarding contracts. Advance notice of all procurement plans exceeding appropriate thresholds must be advertised in the *Official Journal* of the EU, stating whether the call for tender is open or closed. Results of calls for tenders naming the successful bidders must also be declared in the *OJ*.

Under the open procedure, tenders can be accepted for up to 52 days from the despatch of details to the applicant firm. For restricted and negotiated procedures the deadline is 37 days from despatch of details, or 40 days from the issue of a written invitation to bid.

Finding public sector opportunities

You can subscribe to the *Official Journal* directly via HMSO, or visit a European Information Centre (EIC). The address of your nearest EIC can be obtained from the DTI. All EICs stock the *OJ*. Moreover, increasing numbers of Chambers of Commerce and trade associations carry the *Official Journal* for use by their members. European Information Centres also subscribe to 'Tenders Electronic Daily' (TED), the EU's computerised information system. Tender opportunities taken from TED feed into the DTI's Export Intelligence Service (see Chapter 3).

VAT on EU exports

This has been dealt with on pages 107–8, VAT and European Union customers.

Chapter 15
Selling to North America

The North American Free Trade Agreement (NAFTA) is unique in that it brings together two of the world's most affluent nations (Canada and the USA) with Mexico, a poor and economically under-developed country. It took effect on 1 January 1994 and will elimi-nate all tariffs and trade obstacles between member countries by the year 2009: internal tariffs on a large number of product categories were removed at once.

NAFTA has a population of 363 million, making it one of the most important economic trading areas in the world. Common tech-nical product standards are being introduced, so that standards applied by any one NAFTA country will be acceptable throughout the area. Thus, you will only have to meet one set of standards for the entire NAFTA market. Since NAFTA is a free trade zone rather than a Common Market, each member nation continues to determine and impose its own particular set of tariffs against non-NAFTA coun-tries (rather than there existing a common external tariff as with the EU) and there are stringent 'local content' rules to prevent non-NAFTA firms assembling goods in Mexico and hence avoiding US and Canadian tariffs and quotas. Third country products imported into one country cannot be re-exported to other members as if they were domestically produced goods *unless* certain minimum percent-ages of their manufacturing costs have been incurred in the importing nation. For Canada and the USA the figure is 50 per cent; for Mexico the local content requirement can be as high as 80 per cent.

Formation of NAFTA has created the need for additional docu-mentation when moving goods imported from outside NAFTA from one member country to another. An extra certificate of origin is required, drawback (see page 110) is available to importers who re-export items to other NAFTA nations, and a new NAFTA-wide carnet has been developed.

The United States

The USA is the world's largest import market, presenting exporters with opportunities to sell every conceivable type of product. Consumer characteristics and preferences vary from region to region, so careful research into local tastes in the areas in which you hope to do business is invariably required. The nation has a population of around 255 million, spread over a geographical area twice the size of the European Union countries combined. Three-quarters of all US citizens live in cities; 25 US conurbations have populations in excess of 1.5 million. New York (including northern New Jersey) has 18 million people and Los Angeles 14.5 million. Population is growing fastest in southern and western states, and slowest in the northeast. It is important to realise that each US region has its own distinct climate, industrial structure and pattern of consumer preferences. The US population can be roughly categorised as 20 per cent poor and 20 per cent affluent, with the rest in the middle.

Key points to bear in mind when selling to the USA are that:

- inland transport costs are substantial given the long distances between many of the major conurbations (over 75 per cent of all US citizens live in towns and cities);
- climatic conditions differ enormously between north and south;
- the country is perhaps the most litigious in the world. It has more lawyers per 100,000 head of population than any other nation and resort to the law to settle commercial disputes is commonplace;
- business people tend to behave less formally than in many other nations, and much business is discussed over meals and at social occasions.

The USA is well served by directories which you can use to find buyers. Among the more important are the *Directory of United States Importers* and the *International Directory of Importers* (publishers are listed under *Useful Addresses*, see 181). Newman Books publish a series of directories under the title *Chain Store Guides of the USA*, giving company profiles for various retail sectors. Also, there are numerous industry specific directories and directories of trade associations, agents, wholesalers and retail stores. See *Selling to America* by Marianne Willingham (Kogan Page) for information on these.

You can obtain information on how much of your product category is entering the USA by contacting the Foreign Trade

Department of the US Bureau of Census, quoting the relevant HS code (Harmonised Description and Coding System).

Structure of the population

The USA is a nation of immigrants, and the overwhelming bulk of the population can trace their origins to a specific foreign country within the last half dozen generations. About 23 per cent of all Americans claim their ancestry to be German, 16 per cent Irish, 13 per cent English, 10 per cent African and 6 per cent Italian. Other significant groupings are Mexican (5 per cent) and French, Polish and American Indian (4 per cent each). Extensive immigration has occurred over the last quarter century (the highest since the 1890s).

Twelve per cent of US residents are black and nearly 10 per cent Hispanic. In California about 10 per cent of the population are of Asian extraction and 25 per cent Hispanic. In total, there are around 20 million Hispanic US citizens (originally from Latin America) and their numbers are growing. Hispanics could be the biggest US minority group by the end of the decade. Large numbers of Spanish-speaking Americans live in New York, Los Angeles, Chicago, Miami and California. Spanish language advertising is common in these places.

The American population is ageing, due to the dual effects of a decline in the birth rate and an increase in life expectancy. Today, less than a quarter of all US citizens are under 18 years of age, compared with 36 per cent in 1960. The number of people over 65 doubled over the same period. It is predicted that about 14 per cent of the population will be 65 or more by the end of the century. Already this has led to big demands for products typically consumed by the older person (pharmaceuticals and certain types of household appliance, for example). The black population is much younger than the white on average, and is growing twice as quickly. Six in ten US citizens belong to an organised religious group. About half of these people are Protestant; 40 per cent are Roman Catholic. Nevertheless, there is an increasing divorce rate and a smaller average household size. In 1960 about 75 per cent of all American families were headed by married couples. Today, the figure is barely 50 per cent.

Using an agent

Because of America's vast size and the many regional variations in consumer taste, a regional approach to selling is normally required. Hence, most exporters to the USA find that they need to engage local rather than national agents. It is most unlikely that a single representative will have the expertise and/or capability to handle a product throughout the entire US market. Agency agreements are governed by the general law of contract; there is no Federal legislation on the subject although many states have particular rules on agency termination and compensation. Great care is needed when drafting agency (or distribution) agreements since any contract to fix resale prices, impose territorial restrictions or handle competing products has the potential to violate US anti-trust legislation. Aggrieved parties are permitted to sue for three times the level of actual damages incurred.

State and Federal requirements

Each of the USA's 50 states, plus the District of Colombia, has its own set of commercial laws. Additionally, there are Federal laws that apply throughout the country. This results in great complexity and the need to take full account of legal factors when marketing your product. Also, US lawyers work on a no-win no-fee basis thus creating incentives for aggrieved parties to seek legal redress (each side normally bears its own costs regardless of the outcome of the case). State *and* Federal laws extend to product safety and quality requirements, competition, advertising and sales promotion, and banking and finance. Distributors are jointly liable with importers and original manufacturers for damages resulting from defective products, but they typically include clauses in their contracts with suppliers that explicitly pass back liability. In general, liability for damages caused by defective products is very strict in this country. Note, in particular, that:

- it has been held in US test cases that the user of a defective product (not just the purchaser) may sue the supplier even if the supplier was not at fault, provided the goods were the cause of loss;
- US law treats an instruction manual as an extension of a product. Manufacturers have a duty to instruct purchasers or users on how to use a product safely. Poorly drafted instructions can result in the supplier being sued. Service manuals, labels and even sales brochures may all be considered part of a product;
- suppliers are required to warn users not only about potential hazards involved in the use of a certain product but also about the dangers inherent in foreseeable *misuse* of the item;
- manufacturers are obliged to revise product support literature in response to reports of injury caused by the product.

Misleading advertising is illegal under Federal law. This means 'false representations' (express or implied) and/or failing to disclose misleading facts. The rules are stringent, so that:

- liability arises even if there is no proof that any consumers were actually deceived by a false representation;
- literal truth is no defence to an accusation of misleading advertising if the overall representation conveys a false impression, nor is it a defence to argue that the advertiser was not aware of the deception. However, insignificant false representations unlikely to affect purchasing decisions are not actionable. Also, the use of exaggerations, superlatives and subjective opinions to describe an item are perfectly acceptable. Rules on the acceptability of comparative advertising vary from state to state, and expert advice is necessary on this matter.

Trade marks can but need not be registered in order to enjoy legal protection. All that is required is positive proof of first use. A registered trade mark that is dormant for two years can be challenged by a competing business.

Visiting the market

It used to be the case that all foreigners needed a visa before they were allowed to visit the USA. Today, however, UK nationals plus those of 20 other countries may use the 'visa waiver program', provided their stay is for less than 90 days. This means that you can enter the country without first having obtained a visa from the US Embassy as long as you hold a valid passport, have a round-trip transport ticket issued by a carrier authorised by the US Immigration Department, and can provide proof that you will be financially solvent while in the US. Otherwise, you must apply for a non-immigrant visa from the US Embassy.

US imports

The European Union provides nearly a fifth of all US imports and there is significant demand for British goods. Main imports are automotive products, machinery, clothing and footwear, and foodstuffs. The most accessible and fastest growing import sectors in the mid-1990s include automotive products; clothing and textiles; cosmetics, toiletries and fashion accessories; agricultural equipment; giftware; and sports and leisure items.

Public sector buying is important, contributing nearly 20 per cent to GDP (15 per cent of the US labour force works for the government). However, it is difficult to sell to US Federal government agencies because of restrictions imposed by the 'Buy America Act' which prohibits Federal bodies from purchasing foreign goods if local substitutes are available at no more than 6 per cent above the cost of the imports (12 per cent for small businesses or suppliers in areas of high unemployment). Local government is not subject to the Act, but many states have comparable legislation. Big department and chain stores purchase large quantities of imports, as do the major mail-order houses. All have buying offices in other countries.

Most imports can enter the US without restriction, although quotas apply to some products. Quotas may specify an absolute upper limit or impose higher rates of tariff once a certain volume of imports of the goods has been exceeded. Critics of US foreign trade policy some-times allege that technical product safety standards and food and drug legislation are used as *de facto* non-tariff barriers for certain types of goods. All imported items must be marked with the country of origin, unless such marking would physically damage the product.

It is unlawful to import into the USA articles bearing a brand name or other trade mark already owned by a US firm, unless the trade mark owner has given permission. US Customs will deny entry to such items provided the US owner has registered the brand name or trade mark with the Commissioner of Customs.

All retail packages imported into the USA must be marked indeli-bly with the name of the country of origin in English. The country of origin must also be stated on the retail packages of all imported goods. Certain products (notably clothing) have to carry a declara-tion of country of origin on the items themselves. An additional duty of 10 per cent of the value of the imported items may be imposed if they are not properly marked. If articles are 'commingled', that is if items subject to different rates of duty are packed together in such a manner that the quantity and value of each class of article cannot be identified within a package, then the highest rate of duty applicable to any item within the commingled package will be applied to the entire commingled lot.

A comprehensive guide to these and other requirements, entitled *Importing into the United States*, is published by the Department of the Treasury, US Customs Service. This lists the precise information to be included in commercial invoices and the special additional information required for certain categories of product (for a list of the classes of item for which extra information is necessary see *Selling to America* by Marianne Willingham (Kogan Page)).

Customs entry
On arrival at a US destination (or within five days thereafter) the importer has to complete a customs form and provide a commercial

invoice (in English) and evidence of right to make entry. The latter is satisfied via a bill of lading or air waybill, plus a 'carrier's certificate' issued by the carrier attesting that a named person is the owner or consignee. Goods will only be released to the person specified on the carrier's certificate.

There are 165 free trade zones (FTZs) in the USA where goods may be held for *unlimited periods* while they are processed and/or await favourable market opportunities. Also, goods may be fully displayed and exhibited within a zone. Bonded warehouses are available at all main US entry points, offering duty-free storage for up to five years (goods may be transferred to an FTZ at any time within this period). No manufacturing is allowed in bonded warehouses, but items may be sorted, repackaged or otherwise changed in form without their being manufactured. A bonded warehouse could, in practice, be a section of a US business's own warehouse.

Import duty is levied on FOB (free on board) prices or, if these cannot be computed from the available information, the FOB value of imports of identical goods from other exporting firms. If there are no identical goods, the customs authorities will look at similar (rather than identical) items or, if there are no similar goods, will compute either:

- a 'deductive value', that is an assessment of the likely selling price of the items in the USA; or
- a 'computed value' comprising an estimate of the aggregate worth of all the raw materials, processing and packaging costs, profit margins and general expenses required by the product.

Very often, customs entry is effected by 'customhouse brokers', who have to be licensed by the US customs authorities. Brokers are typically engaged by importers and will complete all necessary documentation, arrange for the payment of import duties and secure the release of the goods. Most US customhouse brokers now operate using Electronic Data Interchange (EDI).

If your customer has engaged a customs broker, the latter may ask you to provide price lists, sales literature, brochures and a breakdown of the inputs to the goods in order to obtain from the US Customs a ruling on the duty classification of the item to be supplied.

Canada

Canada is the seventh largest importer in the world, has an extremely high standard of living and immense natural resources. It covers an area of nearly 10 million sq km, but has a population of just 27 million. The country ranges from the polar ice cap in the north to the wheat regions of the central plains and the industrial areas of the southeast. Forty per cent of the country is forest. The country comprises ten provinces and two 'territories'. Provinces have their own local legislatures; territories are subject to central control. Canada is a bilingual nation (English and French). About 45 per cent of the population are Roman Catholic; 30 per cent are Protestant. A fifth of Canadians are under 15 years of age; 12 per cent are over 65. Forty per cent of Canadians claim British or Irish ancestry, 27 per cent French and 5 per cent German.

French-speaking Quebec has its own distinct society. It is on the eastern seaboard of the country, with coasts on the Hudson and James Bays and the St Lawrence Seaway. Quebec covers an enormous area (1,356,790 sq km) and has a population of six and three-quarter million. A million of them speak English as well as French. Eighty-five per cent of all Canadians live within 320 km of the US border.

Internal distribution

Although Canada is a vast country, internal communications are very good. There are three major regional airlines plus around 75 local air services. The road network is extensive and covers vast distances (the west-east Trans-Canada Highway is 8,000 km long). Goods can normally be transported to any major Canadian city by road within three days of importation at a sea port, or within five hours' flying time by air. Rail traffic is declining; certain services have disappeared entirely and others now only run on a weekly or twice weekly basis. Canada has thousands of miles of navigable canals, rivers and seaways and water transport remains a common means for shifting consignments.

Business regulations

As with the USA, the size of the country encourages a regional approach to selling and hence the appointment of agents at local rather than national level. Canada has no Federal laws on agency. Agency agreements are regulated by normal contract law (which itself is based on English law), although each Province has its own specific rules on agency. Contact the DTI for further information on this matter.

Trade marks do not have to be registered in order to enjoy legal protection, but registration is advisable. Registration confers protection for a 15-year (renewable) period.

Canada's Federal Competition Act 1985 requires all advertisements to be truthful. Otherwise, Canadian advertising is regulated at the Provincial level, with each region having its own laws on misleading claims. Further information is available from the Canadian Advertising Foundation.

Customs entry

European Union exports may enter Canada at the country's lowest rates of tariff, provided at least half the costs of their production have been incurred in nations entitled to benefit from the lowest rates of tariff. The latter is imposed on the transaction value of shipments at FOB (free on board). There are no free ports or zones, although extensive bonded warehouse facilities are available. Goods may be stored in bonded warehouses for up to two years without having to pay import duty. The name of the country of origin must be marked on a wide range of imported items.

Canada has special laws to prevent the dumping of goods in the country at less than their 'normal value'. If dumping is causing or likely to harm local industries supplying comparable items or is holding back the establishment of new businesses able to produce the goods in Canada (as determined by the Canadian Import Tribunal) then special anti-dumping levies are imposed.

Mexico

Mexico has a young population: nearly 40 per cent of its estimated 85 million people are below 15 years of age. There are 12 million households with an average household size of 5.5 persons (extremely high by international standards). Ninety per cent of Mexicans are literate. Most of the population is of mixed European and Indian ancestry. About one in five Mexicans live in Mexico City. The official language is Spanish, although English is widely spoken. Ninety-five per cent of all Mexicans are Roman Catholic. Mexico is a poor country (colossally poor in comparison with its NAFTA partners). Half of all Mexicans live below the poverty line (defined as the income level 15 per cent lower than the national minimum wage). Of these poor people, about 40 per cent live in extreme poverty and cannot afford adequate nourishment.

Eighty-five per cent of Mexico's imports are industrial supplies and capital equipment. Consumer goods account for the remaining 15 per cent. Agriculture contributes just 10 per cent to GDP, but employs a quarter of the working population, typically on small and inefficient farms. Industry accounts for 25 per cent of GDP and 20 per cent of employment. Inflation has been high, averaging 48 per cent annually in the late 1980s and early 1990s. However, growth accelerated in the early 1990s and inflation fell considerably (to 10 per cent in 1993). A further encouraging sign is that although the country has a large balance of payments deficit, most of the growth in imports in the early 1990s was in capital equipment and industrial goods which will eventually increase the country's manufacturing capacity. Exporters to the country typically quote cost, insurance and freight (CIF) export prices in US dollars rather than Mexican currency.

Business regulations
Although Mexican law recognises prior use of a trade mark as evidence of its ownership, trade marks should be registered with the Mexican authorities. Registration is for five years, but if the mark is not used within any period of three years, the registration is automatically cancelled. Renewal of registration is only possible if the owner can prove that the trade mark has been used continuously. If a registration is cancelled, a period of one year must elapse before anyone else can use the trade mark.

A number of restrictions apply to the use of sales promotions in Mexico. You must obtain approval from the Secretary of State for Commerce before offering 'free' goods, as in a 'two for the price of one' offer. Coupons are prohibited unless the consumer can be proved to benefit. Premium offers that are unclear are unlawful.

Visiting the market
European Union nationals do not require a full visa to visit Mexico, but do need either a 'Business Card' or 'Tourist Card'. Holders of Business Cards (appropriate for salespeople, persons wishing to conduct local market research, negotiate with prospective customers, etc) have 90 days from the date of issue in which to begin their visit and may stay for one month. When applying for a Business Card you must describe the purpose of your visit on company headed paper. Flying time from London to Mexico City is about 13 hours.

Communications in Mexico have yet to attain First World standards. Letter delivery takes two to three days in the main cities, longer in rural areas. Half the country's roads are without paving. However, there are international airports in Mexico City, Guadalajaro, Acapulco and Monterrey, plus an excellent system of internal daily scheduled services between commercial centres. There is an extensive rail network linking all major towns in the country.

Business meetings are usually conducted in a formal atmosphere, although business hours vary considerably (many offices close in the early afternoon). English is widely spoken in business circles, although some ability to speak Spanish will be greatly appreciated.

Entering the market

Many firms selling to Mexico open a 'representative office', which can be set up at will provided the country's Foreign Investment Commission is notified within 30 days of establishment. Otherwise, much import business is conducted through agents, the majority of whom are based in Mexico City. There is no specific legislation on agency. Individuals (rather than limited companies) appointed as agents are entitled to regard themselves as employees, and hence to claim the protection of Mexican employment law and severance pay.

Although Mexico has liberalised its import regime considerably over recent years, licences are still required for the importation of certain categories of goods (notably clothing and foodstuffs). Applications for import licences should be made well before the proposed shipment dates of consignments. Once granted, a licence is valid for up to nine months. Certificates of origin are needed for a number of product categories, including textiles, clothing, footwear, toys, electrical machinery, tools and leisure and sporting equipment. Samples may be imported for a period of 12 months under a bond which is refundable on the re-export of the goods. Import duties are assessed on FOB values. Some imported goods are subject to specific tariffs. Details of Mexican import restrictions are available from the Mexico Desk of the DTI.

Chapter 16

Australia, New Zealand and South Africa

Australia and New Zealand are English-speaking countries with close affinities to the UK and, in consequence, large numbers of consumers potentially attracted to British goods. However, Japan and the USA, rather than Britain, are the main external suppliers to both nations. South Africa also has a number of attractions for the UK exporter. A substantial proportion of South Africa's white population is English speaking, and the majority of the country's black people have English as either their first or second tongue. Even among the Afrikaner population, business may always be conducted in English.

Management style in South Africa is essentially similar to that found in the UK and, compared to other African countries, it is relatively easy to get paid. Technical and quality standards are based on UK and US norms, and laws on contract, patents and other intellectual property are basically the same as in Britain. The country's business services infrastructure is extensive and of a high calibre.

Australia

Founded and developed by European immigrants, Australia today has a population of around 18 million, but a population density of just two persons per square kilometre. Most Australians live on the east and southeast coast of the country, the vast size of which has two major implications for exporters:

1. The need to appoint different agents in different regions (or an agent with nationwide representation).
2. The advisability of shipping exports to several Australian ports, rather than to a single port followed by time-consuming and expensive transportation across the Continent.

Not surprisingly, for a country so large, air transport is a critically important means for transporting goods. Railways and main roads link all Australia's major cities and there are extensive urban road and rail services.

The nation comprises six regions, each with its own government. New South Wales contains Canberra (the country's capital) and has a population of about 6 million. The Northern Territory, in contrast, has barely 160,000 people (of which 75,000 live in Darwin, the state capital) despite its enormous size. Queensland has a population of 3 million, South Australia 1.5 million, Victoria 4.4 million, and Western Australia (which covers an area larger than all Western Europe) 1.6 million. Sixty per cent of Australians have British ancestry, although since the early 1970s about half of all new immigrants have come from Asia. Australians increasingly think of themselves as belonging to an 'Asian' country, even though consumption patterns follow essentially European norms. The majority of Australians are Protestants, although there is a substantial Catholic minority and all other major religions are represented.

Australia has vast natural resources and a diverse industrial base. Per capita GDP is comparable to those of West European countries and is the second highest in Asia after Japan. Aboriginal rights are currently a major factor in Australian politics: the indigenous population has far lower living standards than the rest.

Business regulations

Trade marks are protected by common law and by the country's 1955 Trade Marks Act, which created a mechanism for formal registration. To qualify for protection a mark must be capable of distinguishing the product, but not be wholly descriptive, scandalous or deceptive. Registration is for seven years in the first instance, renewable for 14-year periods. Marks can be deregistered if they are not used for three years.

There is no special law of agency in Australia. Exclusive distributorship arrangements are unlawful if they inhibit competition. If you enter into an exclusive agreement with an Australian distributor, you need to be able to show that the practice benefits the public. Australian advertising is regulated by the country's 1974 Trade Practices Act under which any advertisement that has the capacity to mislead is unlawful regardless of whether anyone was actually misled or incurred damage. It is also no defence to say that you did not intend to mislead. Voluntary codes of practice govern the advertising of various categories of products. For details contact the Media Council of Australia.

Entry to the market

Traditionally a highly protectionist country, Australia has relaxed its import control regulations considerably over recent years. Tariffs currently average 10 to 15 per cent, the highest of the world's developed countries, but low compared with most nations in the Pacific Rim. Prior to the conclusion of the Uruguay Round of the GATT negotiations, Australia imposed quotas against textiles, clothing and footwear, motor vehicles and any items from specified developing countries. These are now being phased out. Import licences are still required for certain categories of capital equipment (notably heavy vehicles and materials handling apparatus). Non-tariff barriers exist in relation to technical standards, testing requirements, labelling and certification.

Tariff-free entry is available to Australian importers able to demonstrate that local industry cannot produce the imported goods. In this case a Certificate of Origin is required plus a statement that at least half the value of the goods is represented by labour and/or materials of a country recognised to receive the concession. Otherwise, tariffs are usually computed on FOB (free on board) value at the port of embarkation (or relevant inland loading point for means of transport other than ocean shipping). FOB values and ancillary charges need to be shown separately on commercial invoices. It is also necessary to record goods shipped 'on consignment' as distinct invoice items. ('On consignment' deliveries are shipments sent to an agent, who warehouses and sells them on the best terms possible – remitting the proceeds back to the exporter at the moments of sale.) Samples may be imported under an ATA carnet. There are no freeports or free zones in Australia.

Australian legislation enables local firms to petition for an official enquiry into allegations that foreign goods have been dumped within the country. The enquiry will consider whether the imports are being sold at a price lower than in the supplying country or their 'normal' value, or have been subsidised by a foreign government. 'Normal' value could be taken as the selling price in a third country, or the price in the exporter's home nation plus transport and distribution charges plus a fair profit margin.

Visas are required of all visitors to this country, including those from the UK. There are two types of visa: visitor and business. The duration of a business visa varies according to the purpose of the trip.

Packaging and labelling

Certain products (notably food and beverages, textiles, electrical appliances, jewellery and medicinal products) must carry, in English, a trade description and statement of country of origin and composition on both the goods themselves and on interior packaging. Restrictions on packaging apply to foodstuffs, household chemicals and a number of other import categories. Goods failing to satisfy these requirements will be warehoused until they are met.

Packaging that contains hay or straw is forbidden unless a special permit has been obtained from the Directorate of Quarantine of the Australian Department of Health. Wood used for packing cases and pallets has to be treated (by fumigation, chemical impregnation or immersion) in a manner acceptable to the Australian authorities. If wooden packing cases or pallets are used then a separate 'Certificate of Packing' must be included with the other shipping documents accompanying the consignment. The certificate itself need be little more than a typed statement on company headed paper detailing the precise method of treatment. Australian rules on marking and packaging are strictly enforced, and the regulations are extensive and detailed. The DTI will provide you with further information on these matters.

New Zealand

New Zealand comprises two main islands: North Island which contains the country's capital (Wellington, population 326,000) plus the largest city, Auckland (865,000); and South Island which contains one-third of New Zealand's 3.4 million population. Eighty per cent of New Zealand's population are of European origin; 13 per cent are Maoris; 4 per cent are Pacific Islanders. Most of New Zealand's foreign trade is with Australia, with which a free trade agreement came into operation in 1995. Main imports into New Zealand are motor vehicles, plastic products, machinery and mineral fuels. Although New Zealand is an important *exporter* of agricultural products, agriculture employs less than 10 per cent of the country's labour force and contributes just 7 per cent to its GNP.

A general problem with doing business in New Zealand (and in Australia) in the past has been the country's tendency to experience large swings in its economic fortunes, evidenced by big changes in inflation and rates of economic growth. New Zealand's economy declined sharply in the 1970s and early 1980s as traditional industries (especially textiles and agricultural equipment) faltered. This forced the government to overhaul the country's extensive state sector, abolish domestic subsidiaries and generally liberalise internal trade. It appears that the measures were successful and prospects for New Zealand are seemingly bright.

New Zealand legislation on advertising is comparable to that of Australia (see above). It is embodied in the country's 1987 Fair Trading Act under which advertisements must 'present an overall truthful impression in every detail'. The Act also prohibits 'misleading conduct and false representations in the course of trade'. Comparative advertising is generally illegal. Unregistered trade marks receive some protection under common law, although registration is advisable. Trade marks involving descriptive words, surnames or geographical terms may not be registered. There is no specific agency legislation in New Zealand. Disputes between agents and principals are resolved through the normal law of contract.

Visas are not required of UK nationals, who may visit New Zealand for up to six months.

Entering the market
There are no freeports or free zones in this country. Import licences are needed for clothing and footwear. Also, all imported clothing and footwear must be marked with the country of origin. This does not apply to other import categories. Samples may be imported under an ATA carnet. Otherwise, full duty is charged on the commercial value of samples, this being refunded on proof of the items leaving the country.

Import duty is normally (but not invariably) imposed on FOB values. A number of imported products are liable to duty at specific (lump sum per item) rather than *ad valorum* (percentage) rates. Dumping is prohibited under New Zealand's 1988 Dumping and Countervailing Duties Act, which enables the New Zealand customs authorities to impose special taxes on dumped items adversely affecting local producers.

You are not allowed to use hay or straw when packaging goods for export to this country, and rules on the use of wooden packaging materials are strict. Any shipments suspected of being packaged in infected timber will be fumigated at the exporter's expense. For consignments shipped in non-wooden cases, the accompanying commercial invoice must carry the words 'No wooden packaging has been used'.

South Africa

The Republic of South Africa dominates business in the southern part of the African continent. Founded on mining, the South African economy has diverse industries, abundant natural resources and is self-sufficient in food. South Africa is the world's largest producer and exporter of gold and diamonds and possesses extensive deposits of platinum, chromium, manganese and other valuable ores. Nevertheless, manufacturing is the biggest sector of the economy, contributing 25 per cent of the country's GDP. Machinery and transport comprise the major components of manufactured output (18 per cent of the total), followed by agriculture and food processing (13 per cent). Accordingly, South Africa can represent a lucrative market for the export of a wide range of consumer and industrial goods. Germany provides about 20 per cent of the country's imports; the UK, the USA and Japan supply about 11 per cent each, and Italy 5 per cent; the main import markets are for machinery, transport and other equipment, chemicals and oil.

Abandonment of apartheid has led to the establishment of numerous trading links with other parts of the continent. South African trade with the rest of Africa south of the Sahara rose by 40 per cent in 1989, and around 20 per cent annually in the early 1990s. South Africa, Swaziland, Botswana, Lesotho and Namibia have formed the Southern Africa Customs Union, with free movement of goods and a common external tariff.

Nature of the market

The country is a hotchpotch of races, cultures, distribution and purchasing systems, lifestyles and consumer perspectives. Hence, you need to tailor your marketing campaigns to reach multiple markets and appeal to widely disparate groups of customers. Important differences exist between consumers in urban and rural areas, in townships and hostel neighbourhoods, between people in the north and south of the country, among whites of disparate European origins, blacks in various tribal districts and between the emerging black middle class and the financially better-off sections of the mixed race community.

According to the Republic's Central Statistical Service, 72 per cent of South Africa's 38.5 million population are black, 14 per cent white, 10.5 per cent Coloured (mixed race) and 3 per cent Asian. Eighty-five per cent of Coloureds reside in the Cape peninsula; 80 per cent of Asians (nearly all of whom are of Indian descent) live in and around Natal. Forty per cent of blacks, 92 per cent of whites and

165

95 per cent of Asians are urbanised. Ninety per cent of the urban population is to be found in Pretoria, Johannesburg, Port Elizabeth, Cape Town and Durban. At present, most urbanised blacks reside in black townships *alongside* major white urban centres rather than inside the big cities. Overall, the population is extremely young: 50 per cent are under 18 years of age, just 4 per cent over 65. There are nine main languages, Xhosa, Zulu and Sesotho being the most widely spoken. Afrikaans and English are the languages of government. Thirty per cent of the population is illiterate.

The destruction of apartheid has led to mass movements of blacks from traditional homelands to metropolitan areas. As more and more blacks acquire permanent residences and increased incomes they are beginning to purchase dishwashers, microwaves, vacuum cleaners, washing machines, colour televisions, etc, creating a new *racially integrated* market that obliges advertisers to devise cross-cultural, non-racial campaigns attractive to all ethnic categories. Quality, price and product characteristic requirements are changing in line with developments in the socio-economic structure of the nation, with consequent implications for product positioning, distribution and the form and content of promotional campaigns.

There is a United Kingdom Southern Africa Business Association (UKSABA) which, in conjunction with the DTI, has identified a number of product categories considered to offer special opportunities to UK firms, namely, industrial electronics, health care and telecommunications equipment, machine tools, tourism services, educational technology, computer software, office equipment, and items related to general engineering. However, the distribution of personal income is extremely unequal in this nation. At the time of writing, whites (who account for just 14 per cent of the population) receive about 55 per cent of aggregate personal income, blacks 35 per cent (having risen from 26 per cent in 1970). The wage gap between blacks and whites in comparable jobs averages 14 per cent (in 1970 it was 75 per cent). On average, white employees earn between 3.5 and 5 times the wage of black workers, depending on industry sector. Also, black unemployment is enormous (possibly as high as 25 per cent of the workforce).

Consumer characteristics

South African consumers are characterised by their racial, linguistic and cultural diversity. There is a multiplicity of ethnic groupings and a distinct urban-rural polarisation. The country has First, Second and Third World consumers and a huge range of product needs. Among whites, living standards vary from levels comparable to those of the most affluent residents of Western Europe and the USA through to modest incomes (which, nevertheless, are substantial relative to those of most black Africans) for the increasing numbers of white unemployed. Many black South Africans live in dire poverty, especially in rural areas that are in effect agrarian economies operating quite independently of the country as a whole.

The emerging consumer market in South Africa is young, urban and black, with non-white South Africans now accounting for approximately 60 per cent of all consumer expenditure. Two-thirds of all food and clothing sales are to black consumers. A third of transportation spending is attributable to blacks, plus 22 per cent of all insurance purchases. Electrification of the countryside is greatly increasing the demand for household consumer durables among black households. Illiteracy among the black population is a major problem for businesses seeking to promote their goods in the black townships and in rural areas.

Marketing services

Considering the ethnic diversity of the country and its numerous niche markets, most exporters to South Africa rely heavily on specialist intermediaries and advisers when marketing their products. South Africa's advertising industry has an infrastructure equal in sophistication to that of any developed country. Virtually all the multinational advertising agencies now operate in South Africa, pursuing the lucrative business flowing from multinational clients currently re-establishing themselves in the South African market. Also, there are numerous local agencies (many of which have arrangements with the multinationals) ranging from specialist, creative hotshops to large, full-service firms. Not surprisingly, South African agencies are well versed in the art of multicultural advertising, and adept at tracking the 'likeability' of clients' advertising messages within the various ethnic communities. Great successes have been achieved with advertisements that emphasise the 'cross-over' theme: whites working for black bosses, black people exercising their right to express an opinion, and racial intermingling.

South Africa has no legislation *specifically* pertaining to advertising, except for government regulations forbidding misleading advertisements *vis-à-vis* cosmetics, foodstuffs, medicines and certain harmful substances. A number of South African statutes do impinge upon advertising, however, notably the Trade Marks and Copyright Acts, the Harmful Business Practices Act and the Promotion of Competition

Act, all of which have implications for advertising. Otherwise, legal disputes concerning advertising must be resolved through the courts according to the country's common law system. The South African government cites Sweden as the country it most wants to emulate in relation to media and advertising regulation, using state ombudsmen within a legal framework guaranteeing media freedom.

The country has a broad spectrum of large and small market research companies. All types of research are undertaken: product, services, attitudinal, political opinion polling, advertising effectiveness, etc. Consumer sampling and research tracking studies are being completed in black urban areas, providing continuous feedback on brand awareness, use and how specific brands are perceived by black customers. The problem is to balance the representativeness of the results of research against its costs, since the diversity of the South African market means that market segments can be so small that the cost of researching them becomes prohibitively expensive.

Visiting the market

UK citizens do not require a visa to enter the country. Flying time from London to the main South African cities is about 13 hours. Within South Africa the distances between commercial centres are immense, and air travel is usually required (all cities can be accessed from Cape Town via a two-hour flight). A road journey from Cape Town to Durban takes 18 hours on average; by rail it can take up to 40 hours.

Exhibiting

The country has the best exhibition centres and organisation in all of southern Africa, notably in Sun City in Bophuthatswana. Hotel tariffs are low compared with other major conference venues, although exhibition services can be poor and public transport to and from exhibition centres is patchy. Durban is the main city hosting exhibitions, followed by Johannesburg and Cape Town. Several new multi-million-pound centres are currently under construction, many with local authority financial backing. Trade exhibitors are attracted by year-round warm weather and excellent pre- and post-exhibition leisure facilities (tours around some of the country's internationally unrivalled game reserves, for instance).

Distribution

Overall, about half of all sales in South Africa pass through both a wholesaler and a retailer before reaching the final customer; 40 per cent go from manufacturer to retailer, 5 per cent direct to the customer. In view of remaining political uncertainties, foreign companies typically choose to appoint local agents to arrange the distribution of their products. A high proportion of the white, Asian and mixed race communities can be reached through a few city stores; conversely, a huge distribution effort is needed to reach a comparable percentage of the black population. Detergents, for example, are sold to whites through around 825 stores; to blacks through over 30,000 outlets. There is intense brand competition at the top end of the market and retailers have to be persuaded to devote shelf space to new items.

As target market segments are broadened to encompass all ethnic groups and, in particular, lower income consumers, distribution has to be extended to include village outlets as well as city supermarkets and major chains. Lower value packaging is increasingly appropriate. In the black townships there are numerous 'shops' consisting simply of a converted portion of a private house stocking and selling a few essential products needed by the immediate neighbourhood. These outlets are open 24 hours a day and carry only the most popular brands. Hence, it can be *extremely* difficult for new brands to enter this important distribution system. Also, supplying firms lose all control over presentation and final selling prices. Another problem for supplying firms trying to access this kind of ad hoc distribution arrangement is the difficulty of gathering sound market research information on consumption patterns, consumer trends, retail turnover, etc.

Market entry

Customs clearance may occur at the port or airport of arrival or at the large inland container terminal in Johannesburg. Goods often enter at a coastal port and are then removed in bond to Johannesburg. Imports are controlled via an import permit system whereby the issue of permits relates to the availability of foreign exchange. Applications for foreign exchange are automatically granted for authorised imports.

All importers need to register with the South African Directorate of Imports and Exports. Tariffs are imposed on FOB values, or at specific rates on particular items. Samples may be imported under the ATA carnet scheme; otherwise, full duty is payable, but will be refunded provided the samples are re-exported within one year of entry.

Chapter 17
Exporting to Japan

Japan is not a country that instantly springs to mind when looking for potential markets for an inexperienced exporter. It is a long way from Europe, has an ancient, unique and – to foreigners – sometimes impenetrable culture, and possesses a notorious reputation for creating non-tariff barriers against imported goods. Yet Japan is one of the most prosperous countries in the world. Its residents have extremely high living standards, consumer expenditures are continuously expanding, and the Japanese people possess a voracious appetite for quality imports. It is undoubtedly true that in the past Japan has been infinitely better at exporting to other nations than at opening up its domestic market to foreign firms, and international outrage over the foreign trade policies of successive Japanese governments has led to the establishment of state supported schemes and institutions dedicated to helping outsiders (including small businesses) sell to Japan.

A variety of import promotion programmes are in operation. 'Buy foreign' campaigns have been initiated among both industrial buyers and final consumers, and import missions and trade fairs have been organised to help foreigners enter the market. In 1989 the government imposed a special consumption tax intended to discriminate in favour of foreign imported luxury products (including furniture, jewellery and high performance motor vehicles). It also encouraged local agents to handle imports and requested exporters to purchase more foreign items.

In 1990 the Japanese government introduced a package of measures intended to boost the import of manufactured goods, including the abolition of tariffs on imported machinery and several hundred other types of product, plus 10 per cent Corporation Tax credits for firms increasing the value of their imports of manufactures by more than 10 per cent per year. Wholesalers and retailers were permitted to create tax-free reserves set aside for the development of markets for manufactured items. Low-interest loans were offered to importing firms. An office of Trade Ombudsman was appointed to investigate complaints of unfair discrimination against imported products.

Complaints can be initiated via foreign Chambers of Commerce or made direct to the Japan External Trade Organisation (JETRO) which has over 80 offices in 60 countries around the world.

JETRO is based in Tokyo, has a worldwide staff of over 1,200 and a network of 77 overseas offices in 57 countries. Each JETRO office is a self-contained information centre on Japanese business and will offer a variety of services which are usually free of charge. Head office has a database of Japanese importers which is networked to foreign branches so that if you register with JETRO in London, your details will be made available to importers in Japan. In addition, JETRO:

- organises 'import fairs' within Japan intended to generate business opportunities for foreign firms;
- collects samples of foreign goods that might interest buyers and sends them to Japan for display at 'New Import Showcases';
- employs on secondment experienced Japanese businessmen (women managers are few and far between in this country) in foreign offices to provide consultation and support services;
- promotes foreign investment on the Japanese mainland;
- gives overseas businesses practical assistance during the initial stages of their operations in Japan, including free access to databases and a help desk staffed by trade specialists.

JETRO publishes a variety of booklets on such matters as using Japanese distribution systems, contact points for business partners within the country, product sector reports and, importantly, the addresses and details of Japanese wholesalers and large retailing companies. Exporters of manufactured goods can obtain similar but more specialised advice from the Japanese Manufactured Imports Promotion Organisation (MIPRO). Further import promotion measures have included the provision of loan guarantees to importers and the establishment of ten 'Foreign Access Zones' near ports and airports, set up to facilitate the entry of imports. Local firms providing help to foreign suppliers using Foreign Access Zones qualify for subsidies and tax incentives. Zones themselves have bonded warehouses and processing facilities.

Professional advice is essential when seeking to enter the Japanese market. The DTI operates a Japan Desk with separate sections for general enquiries, consumer and industrial goods. There is a Japanese Trade Centre in London, a London office of the Japanese Chamber of Commerce, and the British Chamber of Commerce in Japan which is based in Tokyo.

A word of warning

Notwithstanding JETRO's vigorous and undoubtedly honourable efforts to stimulate imports into Japan, it has to be said that exporters continue to complain about unfair barriers to imports created by the Japanese trade authorities. Specific complaints include:

- modification of mandatory technical product standards at very short notice;
- issue of guidelines on product standards to Japanese firms but not to foreigners, and then insisting that the latter meet exactly the same conditions;
- customs officers refusing to give reasons for rejecting the import of specific consignments;
- complex safety testing procedures, with the need to test excessively large samples under excessively arduous conditions. Preshipment testing has not been allowed for certain products. Testing has had to be completed in Japan, and the shortage of qualified inspectors has led to long delays in the testing process;
- the practice of giving product safety acceptance certificates to local Japanese agents rather than to foreign manufacturers, so that if the latter change their agents, the entire testing process has to be repeated.
- collaborative agreements among Japanese firms that create problems for foreign companies wishing to enter the Japanese market and which would be illegal under the monopoly and competition laws of many other nations. Groupings of firms occur via financial links, sharing common suppliers, or through joint control of distribution outlets. These groupings of Japanese businesses (*Keiretsu* as they are called) exert powerful influences on the Japanese economy. Arguably, it would be easier to export to Japan if there were a bigger number of genuinely independent buying firms. Within a *Keiretsu* there are dominant companies, with material supplies and services being exchanged within the group. The system is supplemented by extensive and close-knit subcontracting networks.

The Japanese market

Japan has a population of 124 million. The population growth rate is modest and, in consequence, the average age is rising. About 60 per cent of Japanese males aged 60 to 64 are in employment, as are around a third of those aged 65 to 69. Japanese people are remarkably alike in comparison with the residents of most other economically advanced nations. They are educated in a similar manner, are influenced by the same media, and have similar lifestyles – even in small towns.

Population and economic activity are concentrated on the eastern coast, particularly in the conurbations around Osaka and Tokyo (population 12 million). A 900-km coastal region running southwest from Tokyo contains half Japan's total population and 80 per cent of its manufacturing capacity. The populations of provincial cities are growing, creating lucrative markets for consumer goods. Another trend is for more people to live on city outskirts, thus expanding the suburban consumer market.

Housing is very expensive in Japan. Most Japanese people cannot afford to buy a house until they are in their early forties, so that the average number of people living in each Japanese dwelling is higher (at around three persons) than in most other prosperous nations. Nevertheless, the average size of Japanese households is decreasing year by year and the number of single-person households is increasing sharply. Hence, there is a large and growing market for single-person household items: convenience foods, light furniture, small domestic applicances, etc. An important consequence of the housing shortage (and consequent lack of spending on this item) is that Japanese families frequently look for luxury consumption opportunities outside the home: cars, holidays in expensive hotels, and so on.

The Japanese market is large and (despite recent recessions) extremely prosperous. Per capita GDP is among the highest in the world and, importantly, Japanese consumers are today spending a bigger proportion of national income than at any time in the country's history. The yen is one of the world's strongest currencies, so that imports are an attractive buy. Increasing affluence has been reflected in a shift in spending patterns towards luxury consumer goods, high-tech products, fashion clothing, health care and financial services.

All Japanese socio-economic groups buy household goods in great quantity, except for the lowest income families. Rates of ownership of particular consumer durables do not vary significantly between regions. The pattern of spending on clothing is also very similar throughout the country. Japanese households spend a larger percentage of their incomes on foodstuffs than in other developed nations (16 per cent compared with 13 per cent in, for example, the USA), consequent to high prices both for luxury and basic food items (this resulting from inefficient domestic food production and high tariffs on food imports).

High consumer incomes have enabled Japanese citizens to purchase consumer durables and other domestic items to such an extent that only the highest quality and most original products are now in demand. An interesting characteristic of Japanese consumers is their propensity to dispose of consumer durables faster than in the West, and not to purchase second-hand items.

Japan has an unusual demographic structure in that it has large proportions in both the young *and* old age brackets relative to other countries. It has the highest life expectancy in the world (76 for men and 83 for women), due perhaps to the Japanese lifestyle and diet. There are nearly 35 million people aged over 55, representing a large and lucrative 'silver market'. Also, the number of Japanese citizens aged 65 or over is predicted to reach about 30 million by the year 2025. Older Japanese people are relatively free spending compared to the rest of the population, due substantially to savings habits and the widespread operation of occupational pension schemes – resulting in very few Japanese senior citizens having to rely on their children for financial support (less than 3 per cent of those aged 65 or over according to the Japanese Statistical Bureau) although over half of them share premises with their children. Senior citizens are big spenders on travel and leisure goods (about 15 per cent of all foreign holidays are taken by those aged over 65).

The female consumer

Many young Japanese women begin work immediately they leave high school and are expected by a large number of firms to resign as soon as they marry (typically in their late twenties) or have children. Prior to marriage, the great majority of females live with their parents and have high disposable incomes. Young women spend large amounts on clothing, leisure goods and travel. However, less than 30 per cent of women aged between 20 and 29 own a car, compared with 65 per cent for males. About three-quarters of all Japanese women re-enter the workforce after they have had children, many working part time. Japan's direct marketing industry may be expected to grow in line with the increase in the number of working women that is currently occurring within the country.

Demand for imported goods

Japan has no oil, so the country's main import category is oil and petroleum products. Next comes foodstuffs and agricultural products, followed by chemicals and textiles. A fifth of Japan's imports come from the USA, while China, Indonesia, Australia, South Korea and Germany each provide about 6 per cent of total imports.

Major markets for imported goods are developing in the fields of computer software, telecommunications equipment, construction equipment and supplies, medical technology, fashion goods (especially clothing) and gourmet foods. Japan imports 60 per cent of its food and is the world's largest importer of food products. The biggest expansions of sales are in the fields of consumer services (insurance, legal services, investment advice, etc), fashion goods and designer items. Affluence is also creating demands for sports and leisure equipment, health and fitness facilities, cultural pursuits and related products, and educational materials.

The Japanese government has announced its intention to reduce the male average working year to 1,800 hours (from its current 2,100 hours) by the end of the decade and to have a five-day working week for everyone. This will greatly increase the demand for leisure products.

The need for quality in the product you put before the Japanese consumer cannot be overemphasised. Japanese people are perhaps the most demanding customers in the world, expecting the highest standards of product quality and customer care. The bottom end of the import market (which is considerable in consequence of the uneven distribution of wealth within the country) is saturated with low-price (but qualitatively sound) items from South Korea, Taiwan and Hong Kong.

Japanese industrial buyers are extremely discerning. The Japanese tradition of life-time employment with a single company means that Japanese executives undergo many horizontal transfers during their careers and acquire first-hand experience of several business functions. Hence, a company's buying department will almost certainly be managed by people with extensive knowledge of marketing, production, company finance and general operations, as well as purchasing. Japanese company buyers, moreover, expect the same reliability, commitment and quality standards from foreign suppliers as is the norm among local Japanese firms.

Technical product standards

Certain mandatory technical standards exactly replicate the characteristics of whatever locally produced Japanese goods happen to be on the market. Items have to conform to these specialised Japanese standards rather than international norms. BSI will provide you with details (see Chapter 3) of particular requirements. For some products (notably pharmaceuticals) Japanese rules insist that safety tests be completed *within* Japan prior to their being marketed, even though the items have already satisfied foreign safety standards more rigorous than those applied in Japan. Hence, extra money has to be spent on replicating previous tests but within Japanese territory. The basic technical standard required of items selling in Japan is the JIS (Japan Industrial Standard) which lays down minimum quality levels (updated every five years) for various products and provides certification for goods that satisfy JIS specifications. Certification (which usually takes from three to six months) enables the supplying firm to mark its output to this effect. Foreign firms may be certificated and will usually increase their sales as a result.

Visiting the market

EU nationals do not require visas to visit Japan. Business travellers may remain in the country for 90 days (although ordinary tourists from the UK can stay for six months). Flying time from London to Tokyo is about 12 hours non-stop, or 17 to 20 hours if a stopover is involved. Travel facilities within Japan are excellent. Domestic airlines serve all parts of the country and Japan's rail network is among the best in the world. However, driving on Japanese roads can be very difficult for foreigners as all road signs are in Japanese script and the roads are extremely crowded (especially in cities). Foreigners wishing to drive in Japan require an International Driving Permit.

Business hours are 9am to 5pm, and meetings are highly formal. An exchange of visiting cards invariably accompanies discussions. Visiting cards are regarded as important and should carry a Japanese translation on one side. The Japanese are punctual, and arriving late for a meeting is likely to offend. Politeness is obligatory. A problem that creates much confusion among foreigners negotiating with Japanese business people is that saying 'no' is considered impolite in this country, so that visitors often assume that a deal has been concluded when this is not actually the case. Confrontations and 'hostile' negotiations hardly ever occur, although Japanese business people are very tough indeed.

Intellectual property

A simple and inexpensive trade mark registration scheme operates. It is wise to register brand names and other trade marks at the earliest opportunity in this country, as the first applicant is entitled to the trade mark irrespective of the fact that it might already have been used within Japan by the rightful owner for several years. This means that an enterprising outsider can register any brand name or other trade mark that the original owner has not bothered to register and then demand payment for granting permission to the latter to continue using the brand name or trade mark on its goods!

Such 'brand piracy' is not uncommon in Japan. Simply being the first firm to use a particular trade mark does *not* confer ownership of it, as is the situation in many other countries: formal registration with the state authorities is required. Registration confers protection for ten years in the first instance, and may be renewed indefinitely thereafter. However, if a brand name or other trade mark is not used in Japan for three consecutive years, another firm can apply to a Japanese court to have the registration cancelled. Trade marks similar to the original should also be registered in order to prevent imitation.

Advertising

Japanese advertising is controlled by the Unjustifiable Premiums and Misleading Representation Act 1977. Under the Act, advertisements must not 'impede competition or treat consumers unjustly'. Misleading advertisements must be withdrawn on the orders of the country's Fair Trade Commission. The latter also approves industry codes of practice on the advertising of various categories of products. These codes contain detailed provisions on how goods may be advertised. For further information on Japanese advertising contact the Japan Advertising Review Organisation.

Distributing your product

The country has domestic distribution systems which, critics allege, respond to Japanese suppliers' pressures to discriminate against imported goods. Systems are complex, costly and bureaucratic. There are several levels in the distribution chain, each link in the chain taking a substantial margin. Intermediaries charge higher commissions to new suppliers (domestic or foreign) than to firms with which they have long-standing relationships. This necessarily discriminates against would-be exporters to the market. Also, a relatively high proportion of distribution outlets are partially or wholly owned by suppliers in comparison with other developed countries.

Long and complicated distribution channels result in the prices of imports rising by three to five times their FOB level (see Chapter 6) prior to their reaching the end consumer. Larger retailers often apply a 100 per cent mark-up. Although the same distribution rules apply to local as well as foreign businesses, critics sometimes allege that the system unfairly discriminates against imports by hoisting their selling prices way above the cost of manufacture. Obviously, the shorter the chain of distribution the better from the exporter's perspective.

Using a *sogo shosha*

An excellent way to enter the Japanese market is to sell to one or more of the giant Japanese trading houses (*sogo shoshas*), which have offices throughout the world (Marubeni alone has over 150) and which deal in a huge variety of products. *Sogo shoshas* will lend money to foreign exporters in exchange for agency rights and will also lend to importing customers. They developed in the early years of the post-Second World War period when Japanese businesses needed to export but possessed little knowledge of foreign markets or export procedures, gradually extending their role from that of simple intermediary to one of direct involvement with exporting firms. A *sogo shosha* might even provide a small business with a complete export management package, including market research, finance, documentation, delivery and insurance.

The use of a *sogo shosha* gives the exporter a ready-made distribution system, accompanied by advice on market trends and customer requirements. It will deal with all aspects of import documentation, warehousing and internal transport, and will be trusted by the Japanese buying public (thus enhancing the imported product's local appeal). The nine biggest *sogo shoshas* handle no less than one-fifth of all Japanese domestic wholesale trade.

The obvious problems with selling through a *sogo shosha* are that (a) you lose all control over product presentation and customer care, and (b) profit margins are lower than if you sold direct. Also, it might not have the specialist knowledge or even interest to promote a particular product effectively. Hence, smaller and more specialised exporters may prefer the services of a *senmon shosha*, of which there are over 10,000. *Senmon shoshas* are perhaps better for specialised products that require expert knowledge of particular niche markets. However, they have fewer financial resources than the *sogo shosha*.

Another possible means for entering the Japanese market is to approach one or more of the 200 or so international trading companies with offices in Japan. These firms are usually concerned with the importation of specialised products, especially capital equipment. They understand European as well as Japanese business methods and have intimate knowledge of Japanese distribution systems. The latter is critically important considering that introducing a new product to the Japanese market can involve lengthy negotiations with a number of intermediaries in various parts of the country. The enormity of the Japanese wholesaling system provides the exporter with a wide choice of options as there will be dozens, if not hundreds, of wholesalers competent to handle the product.

The retailing system

Japan has twice as many retailers per 1,000 population as the USA. A number of factors contribute to this state of affairs. There is obvious consumer demand for a large number of small retail stores, and the layout and architecture of Japanese cities frequently prevents the construction of large, integrated retail units. Another influence is the fact that many Japanese men retire at age 55 and are paid a substantial lump sum rather than an ongoing pension. Opening a small retail outlet is a popular investment for such people.

Japan's estimated one million retail outlets range from large supermarkets and department stores to a multitude of one-person businesses. Japanese retailers expect prompt delivery, substantial assistance from suppliers in promoting the goods, and the option to return slow-moving items without permission. Retailers routinely and conventionally purchase on a 'sale or return' basis. This practice emerged from the tradition of Japanese retail outlets being small and unable to keep unsold stock for long periods. Retailers carry few inventories, consequent to the general lack of storage and warehousing facilities in Japan. Warehouse rents are very high so most storage is done by wholesalers.

Local representation

A common device for arranging local representation in Japan is to open a 'Representative Office'. This is a legally recognised form of business which does not have to register with the local District Legal Affairs Bureau as is the case when setting up a branch. However, Representative Offices cannot engage directly in manufacturing or other operational functions; rather they are restricted to supplying auxiliary services such as advertising, market research, information gathering, etc.

Rules on agency are vague. Agents are perceived as long-term partners of the principal's business rather than as people engaged to supply ad hoc services. Agents normally operate on 10 per cent commission. Contracts can be terminated without indemnity provided a provision to this effect is written into the initial agreement.

It is important to realise that Japan is not a legalistic country. Business is conducted predominantly on the basis of trust rather than litigation, and contract law is far less strict than in the West. There is less than one-tenth the number of lawyers per 1,000 population in Japan than in several other advanced industrial countries. The country has a Civil Code, but this has little to say about business relationships other than when home selling or credit transactions are involved. Contracts are governed essentially by provisions agreed between the parties, and disputes are normally resolved without legal action. This 'custom and practice' approach to the regulation of commerce can lead to imprecision regarding the rights and duties of buyer and seller.

Customs entry

At the time of writing, a small number of products are subject to import quotas. Japanese residents wishing to purchase goods that are subject to quotas must apply to an authorised Japanese bank for an import quota allocation licence, valid (if granted) for six months. Samples may be imported under an ATA carnet or duty free on presentation to the customs authorities of a bank guarantee (provided the items leave Japan within 12 months). Otherwise, samples are liable for full import duty.

Import duty is imposed *ad valorum* on CIF values. Certificates of origin are necessary for some categories of imported items.

Japanese customs officials are notorious for their attention to detail. Small errors in documentation can lead to lengthy (and expensive) delays. Also, a very high proportion of imported goods are physically inspected (up to 60 per cent of items arriving by air).

Useful Addresses

ABC Europ Production
The Universal Register of European
  Exporters
Europ Export Edition GmbH
Berliner Allee 8
Postfach 4034
D-6100 Darmstadt
Germany
Tel: 00 49 6151 33411

Advertisers Annual
Reed Information Services
Windsor Court
East Grinstead House
East Grinstead
West Sussex
RH19 1XA
Tel: 01342 326972

Association of British Chambers of
  Commerce (ABCC)
9 Tufton Street
London
SW1P 3QB
Tel: 0171 222 1555

Association of British Chambers of
  Commerce
Export Marketing Research Scheme
4 Westwood House
Westwood Business Park
Coventry
CV4 8HS
Tel: 01203 694484

Association of British Factors and
  Discounters
1 Northumberland Avenue
Trafalgar Square
London
WC1A 2PX
Tel: 0171 930 9112

Association of Translation Companies
9 Little College Street
London
SW1P 3XS
Tel: 0171 222 0666
Fax: 0171 233 0355

British Airports Authority
  (Air Cargo)
World Cargo Centre
London Heathrow Airport Ltd.
Middlesex
TW6 1JH
Tel: 0181 745 7134

British Chamber of Commerce in
  Japan
16 Kowa Building
9–20 Akaska
1-chome
Minato-ku
Tokyo 107
Japan
Tel: 00 3 505 1734
Fax: 00 3 505 2680

British Exporters Association
16 Dartmouth Street
London
SW1H 9BL
Tel: 0171 222 5419

British International Freight
  Association
Redfern House
Browells Lane
Feltham
Middlesex
TW13 7EP
Tel: 0181 844 2266
Fax: 0181 890 5546

British Standards Institution
2 Park Street
London
W1A 2BS
Tel: 0171 629 9000

Bureau Veritas
42 Weston Street
London
SE1 3QD
Tel: 0171 403 6266

Canadian Advertising Foundation
350 Bloor Street East
Toronto
Ontario M4W 1H5
Canada
Tel: 00 416 9616 311
Fax: 00 416 9617 904

CBD Research Ltd
15 Wickham Road
Beckenham
Kent
BR3 2JS
Tel: 0181 650 7745
Fax: 0181 650 0768

CCN Business Information Ltd
Abbey House
Abbeyfield Road
Lenton
Nottingham
NG7 2SW
Tel: 0115 986 3864

Chartered Institute of Marketing
Moor Hall
Cookham
Berkshire
SL6 9QH
Tel: 01628 524922
Fax: 01628 531382

City Business Library
1 Brewer's Hall Garden
London
EC2V 5BX
Tel: 0171 638 8215
Fax: 0171 480 7638

Civil Aviation Authority
Dangerous Goods Section
Aviation House
129 Kingsway
London
WC2B 6NN
Tel: 0171 405 6922

Commission of the European
    Communities
DG1A3
B28, 28 rue Billiard
B-1040 Brussels
Belgium
Tel: 00 32 2 299 0199
Fax: 00 32 2 299 1028

Cotecna Inspection Ltd
Hounslow House
730 London Road
Hounslow
Middlesex
TW3 1PD
Tel: 0181 577 3911
Fax: 0181 570 8128

Croner Publications Ltd
Croner House
London Road
Kingston upon Thames
Surrey
KT2 6SR
Tel: 0181 547 3333

Dataline
Reuters Ltd
85 Fleet Street
London
EC4P 4AJ
Tel: 0171 250 1122

Department of the Treasury
US Customs Service
Superintendent of Documents
Government Printing Office
Washington DC 20226
USA
Tel: 00 202 783 3238

Dialog Information Services (UK)
PO BOX 188
Abingdon
Oxfordshire
OX1 5AX
Tel: 01865 732075

Direct Marketing Association
Haymarket House
1 Oxendon Street
London
SW1Y 4EE
Tel: 0171 321 2525

Directory of United States Importers
Journal of Commerce
445 Marshall Street
Philipsburg
NJ 08865
USA
Tel: 00 1 800 222 0356

Dun and Bradstreet International
    Ltd
Holmers Farm Way
High Wycombe
Buckinghamshire
HP12 4UL
Tel: 01494 422000

ECAC Secretariat
Kingsgate House
66–74 Victoria Street
London
SW1E 6SW
Tel: 0171 215 4943
Fax: 0171 215 2853

ECHO (European Community Host
    Organisation)
177 Rue d'Esch
1471 Luxembourg
Tel: 00 352 488041

ELC International
Sinclair House
The Avenue
London
EC1M 5QU
Tel: 0181 998 8812

Euromonitor Publications Ltd
87–88 Turnmill Street
London
EC1M 5QU
Tel: 0171 251 8024
Fax: 0171 608 3149

Europages
Herold Fachverlag für
    Wirtschaftsinformation
Schleiergasse 18
A-1100 Vienna
Austria
Tel: 00 43 222 262630

European Direct Marketing
    Association
34 rue du gouvernement provisoire
B-1000 Brussels
Belgium
Tel: 00 32 2 2176 309

Europ Production
ABC-Verlagshaus
Berliner Allee 8
Postfach 4034
D-6100 Darmstadt 1
Tel: 00 49 6151 33411
Fax: 00 49 6151 33164

Export Control Enquiry Unit
Department of Trade and Industry
Kingsgate House
66–74 Victoria Street
London
SW1E 6SW
Tel: 0171 815 8070

Export Credits Guarantee
    Department (ECGD)
2 Exchange Tower
PO Box 2200
Harbour Exchange Square
London
E14 9GS
Tel: 0171 512 7000
Fax: 0171 512 7649

Export Licensing Unit
Kingsgate House
66–74 Victoria Street
London
SW1E 6SW
Tel: 0171 215 8070

Export Market Information Library
1 Victoria Street
(Entrance in Abbey Orchard Street)
London
SW1H 0ET
Tel: 0171 215 7877

Fairs and Promotions Branch of DTI
Horseferry Road
London
SW1P 2AG
Tel: 0171 276 2414

Financial Times Company Abstracts
Financial Times Electronic
    Publishing
126 Jermyn Street
London
SW1Y 4UJ
Tel: 0171 925 2323

Graham and Trotman Ltd
66 Wilton Road
London
SW1V 1DE
Tel: 0171 821 1123

HM Customs and Excise
Tariff Classification Section
King's Beam House
Mark Lane
London
EC3R 1HE
Tel: 0171 620 1313

Institute of Directors
116 Pall Mall
London
SW1Y 5ED
Tel: 0171 839 1233

Institute of Export
64 Clifton Street
London
EC2A 4HB
Tel: 0171 247 9812
Fax: 0171 377 5343

Institute of Linguists
24A Highbury Grove
London
N5 2EA
Tel: 0171 359 7445

Institute of Management
Management House
Cottingham Road
Corby
Northamptonshire
NN17 7TT
Tel: 01536 204222

Institute of Packaging
Sysonby Lodge
Nottingham Road
Melton Mowbray
Leicestershire
LE13 0NU
Tel: 01664 500055

Institute of Physical Distribution
   Management
Cottingham Road
Corby
Northamptonshire
NN17 1TT
Tel: 01536 204222

Institute of Practitioners in
   Advertising
44 Belgrave Square
London
SW1X 8QS
Tel: 0171 235 7020

Institute of Sales Promotion
Arena House
66–68 Pentonville Road
London
N1 9HS
Tel: 0171 837 5340

Institute of Translation and
   Interpreting
318a Finchley Road
London
NW3 5HT
Tel: 0171 794 9931

International Chamber of Commerce
103 New Oxford Street
London
WC1A 1QB
Tel: 0171 240 5558

International Directory of Importers
Interdata
1480 Grove Street
Healdsburg
CA 95448
USA
Tel: 00 707 433 3900

Japan Advertising Review
   Organisation
Dentsu–Kosan
3 Building
2–16–17 Ginza, Chuo-ku
Tokyo 104
Japan
Tel: 00 81 354 12811

Japanese Chamber of Commerce
   and Industry
Salisbury House
29 Finsbury Circus
London
EC2M 5QQ
Tel: 0171 628 0069
Fax: 0171 628 0248

Japanese Manufactured Imports
   Promotion Organisation (MIPRO)
As for JETRO

Japan External Trade Organisation
   (JETRO)
Leconfield House
Curzon Street
London
W1Y 7FB
Tel: 0171 493 7226

Japan Trade Centre
As for JETRO

Kompass Publishers
Windsor Court
East Grinstead House
East Grinstead
West Sussex
RH19 1XA
Tel: 01342 326972

Macmillan Directory of
    International Advertisers and
    Agencies
National Register Publishing Co
3004 Glenview Road
Wilmette
Illinois 60091
USA
Tel: 00 1 708 4412210

Manor House Press Ltd
Hill House
McDonald Road (off Highgate Hill)
London
N19 5NA
Tel: 0171 281 6767

Media Council of Australia
186 Blues Point Road
North Sydney
New South Wales 2060
Australia
Tel: 00 61 2 9549776

Ministry of Agriculture, Fisheries
    and Food
Ergan House
17 Smith Square
London
SW1P 3HX
Tel: 0171 238 3000

NCM UK Ltd
New Crown Buildings
Cathays Park
Cardiff
CF1 3PX
Tel: 01222 824000

Newman Books
32 Vauxhall Bridge Road
London
SW1V 2SS
Tel: 0171 973 6402

PIRA
Randalls Road
Leatherhead
Surrey
KT22 7RU
Tel: 01372 376161

Predicasts Europe
8–10 Denman Street
London
W1V 7RF
Tel: 0171 494 3817

Price Waterhouse
Southwark Towers
32 London Bridge Road
London
SE1 9SY
Tel: 0171 939 3000

Reed Information Services Ltd
As for *Advertisers Annual*

Register of Translators and
    Translating Agencies in the UK
Merton Press
58 Wood Lane
Beverley
Humberside
HU17 8BS
Tel: 01482 867901

Research Association for the Paper
    and Board Printing and Packaging
    Association
See PIRA

Road Haulage Association
Roadway House
35 Monument Hill
Weybridge
Surrey
KT13 9RN
Tel: 01932 841515
Fax: 01932 852516

Royal Mail International
52 Grosvenor Gardens
London
SW1W 0AA
Tel: 0171 681 9410

Science Reference Library
25 Southampton Buildings
London
WC2A 1AW
Tel: 0171 323 7454

SITPRO
Venture House
29 Glasshouse Street
London
W1R 5RG

Single Market Enquiries
Tel: 0171 287 1814
Fax: 0171 287 1914
General
Tel: 0171 287 3525

Société Générale de Surveillance
217 London Road
Camberley
GU15 3EY
Tel: 01276 691133
Fax: 01276 686126

Technical Help for Exporters (THE)
BSI
389 Chiswick High Road
London
W4 4AL
Tel: 0171 996 9000

Timber Packaging and Pallet
    Confederation
Heath Street
Tamworth
Staffordshire
B79 7JH
Tel: 01827 52337

Trade Indemnity plc
12–34 Great Eastern Street
London
EC2A 3AX
Tel: 0171 739 4311

Trade Research Publications
2 Wycliffe Grove
Werrington
Peterborough
PE4 5DE
Tel: 01733 573975
Fax: 0171 233 0231

United Kingdom Southern Africa
    Business Association
45 Great Peter Street
London
SW1W 3LT
Tel: 0171 222 0781

US Bureau of Census
Washington DC 20223
USA
Tel: 00 301 763 5200

Index